PRESSED
FLOWER
PICTURES

PRESSED
FLOWER
PICTURES

❋❋❋

Raymond Foster

MEREHURST

Published in 1995 by Merehurst Limited
Ferry House, 51-57 Lacy Road, Putney, London SW15 1PR

© Copyright 1995 Merehurst Limited

ISBN 1-85391-482-7

A catalogue record of this book is available from the British Library.

Edited by Alison Wormleighton
Designed by Clare Clements

Photography by Lu Jeffery, except for the pictures on pages
10, 14, 15, 17, 19, 20, 22, 23, 24, 26, 27, 31, 34, 39, 41, 45, 47, and 48,
which were photographed by James Purssell,
and the pictures on pages 8-9, 28-29 and 50-51,
which were photographed by Juliet Piddington.

Colour separation by Toppan, Singapore
Printed by Toppan, Singapore

**745.
92**

CONTENTS

INTRODUCTION

What other craft, readily available to everybody, is such a joy to pursue?
Anyone can take up making pressed-flower pictures – and be successful
at it too, because stunning effects are so easy to create. Nature's rich
variety of shapes and textures is just waiting to be used.

The artistic impulse is a powerful one; and unlike painting, which requires expensive materials and considerable experience, with pressed flowers you can create flower "paintings", landscapes, still lifes or other attractive pictures very soon. You have a headstart, after all – because your pictures will feature the built-in grace and perfection of nature itself.

If you want to produce a floral landscape, or a woodland scene straight out of a fairy tale, you can do it. If you want to create an original straight out of your imagination, full of movement and vitality, you can do that too. If you prefer to give your work an antique appearance, or if you admire the flower paintings of the Old Masters, with their perfection of form and intricate detail, these too are within your reach.

Age is no bar to success. Children too can become absorbed in the beauty and creativity of this simple craft with its endless possibilities.

To make a start, pick a few buttercups and daisies, or buy a small bunch of larkspurs at a flower stall. Look along a hedgerow, or in any neglected corner of land, for a few attractive leaves. When you get home, press them all between the pages of your phone book. Soon you will have the pleasure of opening the pages and finding that your flowers and leaves have retained their colour and beauty.

Let your imagination run riot. Try out the various flowers and leaves, even the tips and trails and shoots, that may be growing in your garden, or in your window box. Look too among the weeds that sprout barely noticed along the side of a footpath, or on the roadside verge. Some of nature's treasures may have been growing there unheeded, and your discoveries will open up new dimensions of interest, and the opportunity to experiment.

Some flowers are spectacular, while others, though apparently inconsequential, are full of intriguing detail – vegetation comes in all hues, shapes and sizes. Whether you have access to a fine garden or a mere patch of weeds, your plant material, technique and artistic imagination can combine to make pictures to be proud of, and this book shows you how.

Above and opposite
Unconsidered trifles from your garden and a few tufts of moss, or even the common weed flowers to be found almost anywhere, can easily be transformed into a striking picture with a little care and imagination.

INSPIRATION

INSPIRATION

Pressed-flower pictures are on the brink of a huge revival, which is set to outshine even the craft's previous heyday during the Victorian and Edwardian eras. There is no better time to discover the pleasures and satisfactions of this rewarding craft.

Yellow is an obliging colour for the pressed-flower artist, with numerous subtle tints between cream and orange. Even if your flowers fade to white, they can be revitalized by sticking a newly pressed one on top of the old.

Common wild flowers and tendrils, which are often overlooked underfoot. The cheerful yellow of bird's-foot trefoil associates well with the delicately tendrilled green leaves of the tufted vetch.

Today, there are more beautiful varieties of garden plants than ever before, and our wild flowers after a lengthy setback are returning to the countryside in greater and greater strength.

Once you start pressing flowers, you will never be able to look at one in quite the same way again. You will see it not only as a flower or leaf or tendril, but also as a potential part of some beautiful picture. Your mind's eye will make pictures of the hedge bank, the moorland edge or hay meadow, or the weedy verge of some neglected footpath.

Colour

When picking flowers to bring indoors, you will no longer think exclusively in terms of roses or floral displays, because when

you start making pictures, you will begin to see colour in new ways. There will be colour in tiny detail which you had never noticed before, and which you can only hope will survive the pressing and drying process: the cheerful yellow centres of the tiny laundry-white flowers of stitchwort, or the delicate mauve veins of lady's smock.

There will also be exciting new combinations of colours – the mustardy chrome yellow of biting stonecrop, for example, which looks so welcoming against its dove-grey stone wall. (One of the many local names for this pretty little plant is "welcome home husband, though never so drunk".) In your picture, on a smaller scale, you will prize the canary yellow of bird's-foot trefoil, with its brightening touches of orange-red, twining with the transient blue of the tufted vetch. (The bright purple tinge becomes true blue after pressing, though this too disappears in time.) And there are the warm, tawny shades of polyanthus and wallflower, linked by a splash of dark green, almost black foliage to the background of beige.

Colour can lend depth. But even where there are no real colours to use, where there is only white and black, you still have light and shade, foreground and background. Think of the white flowers of the common daisy standing out from the dark lawn like stars; or even the once bright yellow but now faded flowers of celandine beneath the woodland shade of time-darkened pressed leaves. Shades are as important as colours. If (as will invariably happen from time to time) you find that your pressed flowers have lost their brilliance and turned a disappointing brown, don't write them off – learn to appreciate the new colour.

Brown is the colour of nature. It is the warm neutral hue that lies at the centre of red and yellow, of blues with red in them, and of blues with yellow in them. Look for all the subtle shades of brown, from cream through buff and beige and bistre, through ochre and fawn and russet and tawny hazel. Find shades of amber, bronze and chestnut and mahogany. Look closely at shades ranging from rust and cinnamon to puce and amber and sepia and liver, to milk chocolate and coffee. These are the real earth colours.

So when you unscrew the press or lift the pile of books and open the paper, don't throw away the brown flowers in disgust. Use them! Brown goes with almost anything. Try a graded succession of brown flowers along a twining stem, or against an orange autumn leaf. Experiment with placing it next to a larger flower which has retained its own colour, but which includes brown in its makeup. You will see that small as well as brown is beautiful here; it will make the subtle shades in the tiny detail spring to life.

Always keep a selection of small autumn leaves. Maple leaves in particular show an interesting range of shapes and colours. They are easy to store flat in a book or envelope.

Instant renewal
Even flowers that have retained their colour well in the press may lose it gradually if the finished picture is hung in full light – the greater the light intensity, the faster the loss. Direct sunlight, of course, is the worst culprit. If it worries you, and you don't want to tint them, you can always glue on another flower of the same type, either to replace or to reinforce the original faded one. It can enhance the appearance no end.

For instance, celandine will eventually lose its clear, shining yellow in the light and fade to white. It is still very attractive, but you may feel that the picture needs that touch of bright colour. Therefore, you simply stick a freshly pressed celandine on top of the old flower. You will instantly have achieved an intriguing double-flowered effect, with the white petals below enhancing the purity of the bright yellow ones above.

Leaves made to fold along a vein or margin can be used to give your picture the illusion of depth and movement. The leaves used here are bramble, aided by a sprig of Russian vine.

A simple sprig from a garden shrub is an inspirational starting point. The flower you may want to add need not even be from the same bush, provided the rhythm of the picture is enhanced. Already this is an artistic composition.

Form and depth

Symmetry and balance will play an important part in your choice of material, and you will find yourself saving your most symmetrical leaf sprays and your most evenly proportioned flowers for the more formal designs.

A leaf that can be persuaded to fold along the line of its vein often greatly enhances a picture, particularly if it is a two-toned leaf, with a white or yellow, grey-woolly or silvery reverse. Goat willow or sallow leaves are particularly good at doing this, and they also readily curl and fold back a little along their margins, which bestows a similar effect. To a lesser extent, mugwort leaves will do this too, giving a frosted silvery rim to the green upper surface, or a dark green outline to the light-coloured reverse side. The effect on your picture will be to add a third dimension by apparently giving it depth, besides adding the illusion of sunlight striking the foliage from above, or reflecting from below.

Reflected light plays a major part in the artistic use of light and shade, technically known as chiaroscuro, which gives solidity to good paintings. Now is the time to think about this – at the pressing stage rather than later when you come to make your picture, for by then the lines of the leaves will be set, and the possibility of adding depth through this chiaroscuro effect will be gone.

Flower-pressers tend to avoid green leaves as being too ordinary (and not the easiest colour to preserve), and select variations of colour instead, the more striking the better. But by doing so an important element is left out of the picture.

Rhythm and composition

There are said to be three elements in art: emotion, expression, and rhythm. You feel the emotion, you gather your materials together to express that feeling, and you use your artistic sense of rhythm to give it solid reality. Life itself is movement in one form or another, and rhythm is really what makes us feel happy about that movement; what used to be called "good vibrations". The composition of your picture has to be at least related to movement and rhythm. Rhythm is automatically set up between the basic lines of your composition – formed by the curves of petal and stem, or perhaps an exploring trail of flowering creeper – and between those lines of movement and the boundaries of the picture.

Composition is the placing of your material – creating forms, shapes, and empty spaces – and it is worth taking some trouble over. Your picture needs to generate some degree of interest in the eye of the beholder, which should be guided into it, starting perhaps with some bright splash of colour or highlight to act as an eye-catcher. Then the observing eye should be led around and into the depths of your subject, almost as if it were a real landscape, or a real and well-designed garden waiting to be explored.

Symmetry at this stage is not important, but balance is. Try to avoid placing an over-heavy mass on one side. Without a counterbalance you risk leaving a feeling of emptiness on the other side. If you are making a pressed-flower scene rather than merely a group of flowers, the principles of landscape design will be reflected in the picture.

A miniature hill will follow the shape of your material. Whatever your original intentions, a rounded hillock only appears so because you have used round-contoured plants, and a prominently pointed peak will be the result of having used spiky, conifer-like plants.

Composition – the process by which a few odd strips of wood veneer, some silverweed leaves and goatsbeard catkins begin to transform themselves into a believable landscape.

The warmest shades of red, orange and yellow glow with light and seem to thrust themselves into the foreground, but are held firmly in place by the bright green of the leaves in between.

The beautiful and the picturesque

Beauty, of course, is supposed to reside in the eye of the beholder, but fashion has always dictated how beauty is defined. During the so-called Romantic period two hundred years ago, landscape artists in particular began to emphasize certain natural features in order to produce a wild look. On a more practical plane, and by using such natural materials as were available, the landscape designers too sought to develop a particular theme: peaceful, or wild and untamed; mysterious, or grand and imposing.

And so it became fashionable to distinguish between the "beautiful", which was calm and restful, and the "picturesque", which was striking and contrasting. This is where the similarity between landscape gardening and pressed-flower artistry comes in. We too work with natural textures, colours and forms, which possess various characteristics: soaring, creeping, rigid, pliable. Both the wild look and the restful style now have their time-honoured place, and either may set the mood of your picture.

Perspective

During the European Renaissance, artists began to learn about perspective, and gradually mastered the technique of giving their pictures the appearance of depth. They became outwardly more observant, and this perhaps is the great strength, even today, of Western as opposed to Oriental art. Pre-Renaissance scenes by Western artists are often quite charming, and you can always see what it is "supposed to be", but the results do tend to be diagrammatic rather than pictorial. The pictures lack depth.

Obviously, perspective is not essential for the enjoyment of a picture in the way that movement and rhythm, composition and balance are. But it does solidify a scene and make the picture believable. There is no reason why perspective should not be built into your pressed-flower picture, using flowers perhaps of diminishing or increasing size. Light and shade convey a similar effect, with light flowers appearing to approach, and dark ones seeming to recede.

If carefully planned, colour too will give depth, with the "warm" shades of red, yellow and brown seeming to advance, and the "cold" shades of blue, blue-green, and all the palest colours seeming to retreat. Our brains have learned to see things in that way. The blue of a sky can never seem to approach nearer than the foliage and flowers visible against it, but those little bright red flowers that you had intended to stay in that distant field will insist on thrusting themselves forward to intrude on the foreground.

We cannot really escape from perspective, so it is not something to be ignored when making a pressed flower *scene*, as opposed to a design pure and simple. A scene will end up with a horizon, or an assumed horizon (brought about perhaps by the placing of your ground vegetation) whether you intended it or not.

Never forget that the horizon or skyline represents your own, and the viewer's, eye level, and it is the eye level that gives a sense of comparative height and depth. If you are lying on the ground, you will not be able to see very far. The horizon will be very low indeed, and trees and other tall things will tower above it. If you climb a hill, on the other hand, you will see a great deal of foreground in front of the horizon, which will be very high, above even the tallest trees.

So even if the floral scene is quite a simple one, our brains will try to analyse it and decide where the skyline is, which is foreground and which background. If we can't instantly decide these things it makes us feel insecure and a bit annoyed. Look how many people react to purely abstract paintings by saying, "Yes, but what's it supposed to *be*?" They never say that about symmetrical designs!

Creating a horizon

Simply by positioning the root buttress of your tree in a certain place, and by the sweep of your surface vegetation, your drift of flowers, your spray of moss, you are creating a horizon, or eye level. If you are doing a sylvan scene, imagine you are walking through the woods. A horizon that is too high will give the viewer a bird's eye view. With one that is too low, the viewpoint will be similar to that of a mouse. It follows that a low horizon will tend to make objects – trees, flowers, leaves – seem larger. Conversely, a high horizon – a high viewpoint – will have a dwarfing effect.

From the normal human viewpoint, a tree is a tall object. For it to look impressive, or at least realistic, its base should be scarcely below the horizon. If your foreground flowers appear above this point, unless they are supposed to be growing on a little hill, the effect will be similar to those medieval paintings which did not take perspective into account. It may be a beautiful design and it may look very attractive, but it will not be a realistic piece of landscape.

Producing an illusion of depth

Simplicity can help. Many pressed-flower pictures try to cram too much into the available space, so that any effect of depth is lost. The size of the flowers, and their colours too, have a powerful part to play in creating this illusion of depth through perspective.

Just as a bright red flower, placed in what is intended to represent the distance, may spoil the planned effect by insisting instead that it grows in the foreground, white too

One of the simplest of pictures in construction. The gulls are pairs of buddleia leaves which have partially rolled themselves up during storage. The addition of a horizon and a few smudges of colour turns the picture into a seascape with depth. The setting sun is a fleabane flower.

Above The creamy white of Japanese knotweed turns to russet brown, and spiderplant darkens its pale leaves to shades of fawn. But transformed into an exotic flower, both will retain their place in your picture.

Opposite "Exuberant but well-balanced chaos" typifies the Western style of flower painting as well as flower arranging. Included here are rhododendron, delphinium, leopard's-bane, pansies, pelargonium, larkspur, honesty, rosebay willow-herb, bird's-foot trefoil, wild garlic and meadowsweet. Beneath the vase is the merest suggestion of a tabletop, but the perspective still needs to be believable.

may do this, and so may bright yellow. It shouldn't worry us too much, however, because the soft, mellowed shades which are characteristic of pressed and dried flowers are usually content with a background position.

The problem we usually face is one of the flowers fading, and when this happens it too can upset the perspective. A strong foreground can easily be lost, and with it goes the picture's illusion of depth. Sometimes a judicious touch of retinting may be needed to restore a good perspective.

You will often find that one or two large flowers strategically placed will represent the foreground effectively, if there are smaller flowers of a similar colour and shape (not necessarily of the same type) in the receding middle distance. Large, shrubby hypericum flowers, for instance, can front a drift of more distant buttercups, with stunning effect. A solitary clematis flower on an overhanging branch may be used to counterbalance faded crimson crabapple blossoms in the more distant foliage. Even so, artificial colouring is still likely to be needed sooner or later, as different types of flower, though of a similar colour, do not fade to the same degree.

European flower paintings

Having explored the possibilities of landscape, and learned a little about perspective and depth, we can look for inspiration towards the work of famous flower painters of the past.

In the earliest recorded art of Europe, principally that of the ancient Greeks, there were virtually no incursions into the picturesque possibilities of nature. The accent was always on the human, or occasionally the animal – on the perfection of bodily form, on idealized physique and grace of movement both of man and beast. Everything was depicted with a perfection that outshone nature. No naturalistic flower designs are to be seen on surviving artefacts of ancient Europe; plants were never regarded as objects of beauty. When they did appear in works of art, they were idealized and portrayed as a symmetrical design.

Only much later, and gradually, did flowers begin to emerge as subjects in their own right. In the earliest flower paintings they were used merely as objects of religious sacrifice (and perhaps some people who "do the flowers" in church see them in a similar way even today). And up to a few centuries ago Western artists certainly saw flowers as supplementary to their religious subjects. They provided an offering, a garland to adorn them, which was always subordinate to the main theme. It was only during the seventeenth century that flowers were perceived as subjects to be admired for their own sake, and the art of painting flowers began to develop.

Most of these early flower painters concentrated on the flowers themselves, which were often shown without a container. But towards the close of the seventeenth century, it became the fashion to include

The impression of light within a pressed flower picture usually depends upon the transparent individual petals allowing a light-coloured backing to show through. But when the background is dark, to represent shadow, pure opaque colour can also provide a vivid impression of light.

beautiful foliage and a vase in the composition. The flowers became less restricted and began to show the natural eccentricity of their form, with a graceful curve to their stems.

During this period artists in Belgium, Holland, Italy and Spain were increasingly producing masterpieces of flower-painting technique. Their vases tended to be arranged with long stems and overhanging trails, stressing the free and easy growth of the flowers.

During the Victorian era, flower paintings were painstakingly "sweetened" with the petals silkily fragile. They were made to look "prettier" than they actually were. By comparison, earlier studies of flowers look robust rather than delicate. We can emulate a style using real pressed flowers, but we cannot hope to make a petal look more robust or more delicate than it actually is. We can only vary our selection of flowers to suit the style of picture. The flowers themselves do the rest.

Flower painting at the close of Victoria's reign began to take a new direction. A powerful French influence in the form of

Impressionism set painters looking for the subtle interplay of light and translucency of colour. In this rather self-conscious striving to produce a luminous quality, the accent was on capturing an *impression* of light with pure colour. Flowers were painted not merely for themselves, but as a medium with which to express the sensual vibrations of life. This contemplative inner view was strictly Western in its approach and very different from the Oriental brand of inner perception which shows itself in ikebana – the Japanese style of flower arrangement, which follows strict rules – and in Chinese as well as Japanese flower paintings.

Oriental flower paintings

If you have a plentiful supply of showy flowers to arrange, you will seldom be short of the inspiration to make good pictures. But if your stock is more limited, if you find that boring leaves and grasses or small inconsequential flowers outnumber your first-choice selection, you may find the inspiration you are seeking in the East. In China and Japan, though they often use

beautiful flowers, a solitary bamboo or a gnarled twig can be the subject of an outstanding picture.

In China, the art of flower painting attained its peak early, and for a thousand years, between the seventh and the seventeenth centuries, it was pre-eminent in the world. In Japan, the art of flower painting grew later, and was at its best during the sixteenth and seventeenth centuries, coinciding with the development of flower painting in Europe.

The art of the East has always been concerned with the philosophical, contemplative and poetic aspects of life. Eastern flower paintings typically have emphasized the rhythmic movement of nature with all its changes of seasons and moods – the rhythm of life itself. In the West, the approach has been more objective.

Perspective plays little part in Oriental pictures, but there are other time-honoured conventions which have been used to express depth and distance. Notice how many Eastern-style landscape paintings tend to be arranged in distinct tiers, the foreground at the base, the midground in the centre, and distance at the top. Simplicity is always the keynote. A cluttered picture, to the artistic Oriental mind, is wearisome, while empty space allows the imagination full rein.

And so, in purely practical terms, Oriental-style pictures must be basically simple in composition. Having sensed the spirit, the essential characteristic, of the subject, this essence has to be expressed with as few strokes of the brush as possible. With this model as our guide, a pressed-flower picture with an Eastern flavour must also be simple and uncluttered.

A favourite theme recurrent in Chinese paintings involves low, spreading plants combined with tall, soaring ones – as a water lily floating, with bamboo stalks spearing mistily skywards, or reeds as seen by a water fowl swimming on the lake. When you realize what Chinese flower painters in particular have tried to achieve, you will probably conclude that Western flower pictures are in a sense "still-life" paintings by comparison. Superb studies they are, and marvellously executed, but they have never tried to show that essential feeling of life and movement, and the *quality* of living plant growth that typify Eastern flower paintings.

Eastern contemplation on the meaning of life shows itself in the Japanese flower-arranging art of ikebana, where the accent is on uncluttered line rather than mass or colour. The flowers used here are wallflower and delphinium.

A simple drawing is turned into an eighteenth-century Meissen coffeepot by the addition of a traditional pottery design known as "the German flower". In this case it is a chrysanthemum, once salmon-pink but now darkened to coffee brown, associated with apple leaves, goldenrod, and a boss of clover.

Eastern art, in other words, has always aimed to capture the spirit of its subjects rather than an accurate likeness; the inner meaning is more important than physical characteristics. It is an attitude that fits in well to the limitations of the pressed-flower artist, particularly when we try our hand at landscapes. They *have* to be stylized. A trail of moss has to represent a solid hillside, and we have only full-sized sprigs of moss, and full-sized flowers and leaves, with which to represent miniature scenes.

Antique pottery and porcelain

Eastern expertise with watercolours and with brushstroke calligraphy combined

to produce pictures of grace and character which associated well with the silk or flimsy paper that was normally used. But many of the Chinese flower designs to be seen on antique pottery and porcelain are quite breathtaking too. They may be a thousand years old, like those of the Sung or T'ang dynasties, but their patterns are exquisitely dainty.

European pottery and porcelain can be an even richer source of inspiration to the pressed-flower artist. There are the Delft plates, German pots from Meissen and French vases of the Forme Aubert; English Worcesterware too carries beautiful designs. Since the seventeenth century, many European pieces have reflected a strong Eastern influence. Delftware, for instance, often features ikebana-style sprays of chrysanthemums straggling across the surface of the plate.

Ikebana and Japanese flower painting are inseparable. Japanese painters are less concerned than their Chinese counterparts with the essence of the individual flower, more with its meaningful style of growth. The intention of a picture, or a flower arrangement, is often to evoke a mood or recall a memory.

Inspiration from flower arrangements

Flower arranging is always a rich source of inspiration for the pressed-flower artist, whether he looks to the East or the West. In Europe and North America, the traditional and most popular flower arrangement is the "massed" style, in which abundance and profusion of colour set the tone. It always results in something eye-catching, but a sense of balance is very important if the design is to be truly pleasing. Usually those flowers with the heaviest appearance (not necessarily the largest in size) will appear at a reasonably low level. The finer, more delicate and spirelike types will be at the top and the extremities, otherwise the arrangement may seem top-heavy. But, as always, it is mainly a matter of personal taste.

Arrangements which are based on line rather than mass are perhaps more interesting. Sweeping lines have a fresh and vital look about them which suggest that powerful, natural forces are at work. Proportion and balance are even more important in this case, and the whole arrangement needs to be more thoughtfully done. As in Oriental design, simplicity rather than superabundance has to be the rule. Line-based arrangements may be basically vertical or horizontal, or sweeping in a graceful half-moon curve, and all of course will have their counterparts in nature.

If it is normal in the West when creating an arrangement to use as many flowers as are available, crammed together in exuberant but well-balanced chaos, the Eastern way with flowers sometimes seems to work on the principle "the fewer the better". The contrast shows too when one compares the typical Western garden, intended to produce a successional riot of colour, and the traditional Japanese garden, which may display little more than green leaves, or even perhaps a solitary rock amid raked sand, an "island of tranquillity in a sea of disturbed feelings".

Art Trouvé and collage pictures

Art Trouvé – the use of natural or unexpected objects in art – has always been a powerful constituent of ikebana and has become a favourite concept with many Western-style flower arrangers. A weirdly

Even so simple an arrangement as a solitary fern leaf and a sprig of heather needs careful balancing. The twiggy stems of the heather are concealed beneath meadowsweet and a twist of moss.

shaped piece of driftwood is a particular favourite. In ikebana, the favourite non-flower addition is a branch which has been stripped of its bark to produce a similarly grotesque, weatherbeaten appearance, suggesting the harsh vagaries of nature.

Collage pictures which include bulky dried material are closely related to Art Trouvé. They will probably be more subject to the effects of atmospheric moisture after completion, as they cannot readily be rendered airtight like flat-pressed pictures, which can be covered with plastic film or heat-laminated to seal them. Collages can make use of practically anything "trouvé"

An example of Art Trouvé, using a suitably distorted piece of natural bark from the woodpile to form the trunk and limbs of a gnarled bonsai tree in the Japanese tradition. The storm-blasted greenery may include moss, lichen and mugwort leaves, with the addition of any tiny flowers you can find.

in this sense: bark, seedheads, pine cones, bulky lichens and twigs, even animal materials such as snail shells, skulls and feathers. This method of picture-making should be particularly attractive to extravagant artists who want to squander all their material in one gorgeous layout.

Flowers in Art Nouveau and Art Deco

Around the beginning of the twentieth century, the movement known as Art Nouveau represented a desire to escape from the formalities of academic tradition by the use of non-classical forms of plants. It was a revolt of the designer rather than

the flower painter. Art Nouveau designs are freely ornamented within the limits of balance and symmetry, abounding with curves and shunning straight lines. The movement was a matter of design, but it was essentially of a plant nature: its essence was of flowers.

The pressed-flower picture that makes use of symmetry and repetitive design automatically approaches Art Nouveau. The flowers that appear within your designs may recur geometrically, but they will vary according to the whims of nature rather than the strictures of geometry.

The Art Deco movement of the 1920s and

'30s was a sign of the times. All the old restrictions and straitlaced attitudes of the past were being cast off, and everything aimed to be thoroughly modern. Fashionable art was characterized by bold colours and strong lines, and perhaps a rather contrived lack of symmetry. The impact, the sensation, was the important thing. Bold designs in pressed flowers featuring showy petals of tulip, iris and the like are almost bound to carry some faint echo of this unrestrained period.

Kaleidoscopic circles and fans

You have only to arrange a few pressed flowers close together, and you will have made a design. It may be a very attractive design too, but it will probably be a "flat" one. To limit yourself to the simple flat group is rather like making random daubs on a sheet of paper. If you are content with this simple method of grouping, you can modify it by arranging them in a kaleidoscopic circular pattern. You can also always fall back on this idea when you are short of inspiration, particularly if you have a good supply of small and individually inconsequential flowers you would like to use up.

Falling short of the complete kaleidoscopic circle, traditional-shaped fans can be the basis of intriguing designs for the pressed-flower artist. The most ancient fans were those of the Far East, and their original form was a bunch of peacock or pheasant feathers, mounted on a handle. Since those days, palm, bamboo, silk, ivory and many other materials have been put to use. The Japanese in medieval times used a special war-fan for signalling on the field of battle. More peacefully, the Japanese for centuries have used fans in connection with their famous tea ceremony.

Ceremonial fans too were used by ladies of the court. Most of these early Oriental fans were painted with figures and scenes, and ornamented with artificial flowers and long streamers of coloured silk. In Europe they became the vogue during the sixteenth century, and high-born ladies in many a portrait of that period are shown sporting ornate fans of intricately carved ivory. There even grew up a romantic system of code signals between flirts and lovers.

During the succeeding century fan-sticks were often made of mother-of-pearl or tortoiseshell, besides ivory. Between the sticks, parchment or thin kid leather was often employed. The cheapest fans used paper, cut into geometric shapes, while the richest ones were embellished with precious stones, gold and silver.

Lace fans were next to come into fashion, and it is they, perhaps, which most inspire the pressed-flower artist to take a leaf from the old fan-makers' book. Some of the best lace designs were seen in Italy

The kaleidoscope technique is very much in evidence in this design, which would look good beneath the glass top of a small table. The butterflies' wings are monkshood and busy Lizzie (impatiens), while a circle of rosebay willowherb flowers with their curling stems adds to the illusion of whirling flight.

A formal design planned primarily for its striking silhouette. This is one occasion where weeping willow leaves do not look out of place thrusting skywards. The feathery grasses are secured in their bunches each by a small sprig of meadowsweet, while mugwort leaves continue the symmetrical theme at their base.

and France during the eighteenth century, and it is these designs – abstract and geometrical, but flowerlike – that lend themselves best to pressed-flower designs.

One great advantage we have over ivory-carvers, lace-makers, and painters is that we can move our medium about – shapes, colours and all – until we reach a pleasing effect. Serendipity still rules, so it may not be the effect we first had in mind.

If your inspiration is a fan, or if you are employing the kaleidoscope technique, you will need to move your material around symmetrically. But for actual pictures, as opposed to symmetrical designs, balance is more important than symmetry. (If you can visualize your work as a free-standing sculpture instead of a flat picture, it will be obvious that the end result must

look as though it would stand firm by itself, and not fall over.)

Wrought ironwork

For an exercise in pure design, try limiting your materials to trailers of ivy and ivy-leafed toadflax, bindweed, bryony, and the grasses, to evoke the symmetrical balance of ornate wrought iron.

Again, we can look to the past for guidance. During the eighteenth century, the Chinese specialized in delicate wrought-iron panels representing a gnarled tracery of branch and stem, blossom and leaves, set against a background of paper or silk. A favourite subject was the four seasons. By using twining stems and trailing tips, tiny flowers and leaves, the spirit of these can readily be recaptured, and they will be

all the more beautiful for their natural colours. On the other hand, it could be a good way to use up material which has gone dark brown or black. The colour of backing paper or cardboard will be important here, and should be chosen with care.

There is no need, of course, to go to China for your model. The Europeans too have produced delicately graceful examples of wrought ironwork, though here the representation of plant material tends to be rather more formalized and symbolic. A supreme example of European wrought iron, dating back to the Renaissance, features on the main door of Notre Dame Cathedral in Paris. The work seemed to the people of that time to be of such unearthly beauty that for several centuries it was fabled to have been wrought by supernatural hands.

Stylized designs

A marvellous symmetrical–asymmetrical design feature is that strange teardrop-shaped motif known as a cone, typical of the paisley pattern. The shape does bear at least a passing resemblance to a pine cone. It was used in the famous shawls manufactured in the Scottish town of Paisley and elsewhere in Europe during the nineteenth century. The motif was copied from the woollen shawls produced in Kashmir from the fifteenth century, and exported to Europe from the eighteenth century. In India this motif was also used in other textiles, carvings and tiles.

Something similar to the paisley cone, a shape intended to represent flowering trees, is seen in many Indian paintings of the sixteenth and seventeenth centuries. The pictures are often devoted to religious themes such as the earthly life of Krishna, and the rather beautiful trees feature in

The simple design formed by a flowering spray of montbretia, while wholly natural, can be used to dramatic effect as one of the components of a stylized picture.

stylized landscapes which introduce their own interpretation of perspective and depth. The idea can be turned into a very striking pressed-flower picture. The bold, diagrammatic way these trees and figures are represented, and their bright colours, give these paintings something of the look of an Oriental carpet or tapestry.

Many Indian carpets from the same period in history are very distinctive. They are divided into quatrefoils or ogee compartments, each containing a cluster of very natural-looking flowers in a broad range of colours – a gift for the pressed-flower artist in search of ideas.

The five-blossom carpets, often called Khotan carpets, typical of Turkestan in the seventeenth and eighteenth centuries, show traditional patterns that can also readily be simulated using pressed material. They feature characteristic groups of five flowers in once brilliant but now faded shades of red, orange and blue.

Old Chinese carpets often feature floral or leaf patterns, but best perhaps, from our point of view, are Persian carpets from the sixteenth century or thereabouts, with their tiny, intricate detail of trees and flowers in curving patterns of blue, yellow, red, white and black. Some examples from old Persia are known as "vase carpets" because of the highly stylized vases of flowers which feature over and over again in their design.

Far left *Crabapple "Profusion". Apple twigs are too woody to use in a pressed-flat picture, and this one is made from wood veneer-faced paper. The flowers and leaves have been pressed complete in small sprays, with odd flowers and leaves added separately as required.*

Near left *Wild Rose. Rose flowers are best pressed singly, without stems or leaves attached, and reassembled into sprays as required. The flimsy petals should not overlap the stems, which are best trimmed to size and added last.*

Returning to Europe, some of the most popular floral art, while natural in detail, is quite highly stylized in form. Consider the well-known flower portraits of Pierre-Joseph Redouté (1759–1840). He is said to have spent hours arranging his material, and even then he was highly selective in what he depicted and what he omitted. Not a leaf or petal could be allowed to slip out of place to mar the symmetry of the whole; but the process paid off, and his pictures are more popular today than ever. A pressed-flower picture in the style of Redouté is a pressed-flower picture that will sell – and what could be more inspirational than public demand!

Opposite *Made of Japanese wood veneer-covered paper, with rhododendron flowers and goat-willow leaves, this flowering spray is very much a stylized composition, and could equally well represent a tree in the bonsai tradition.*

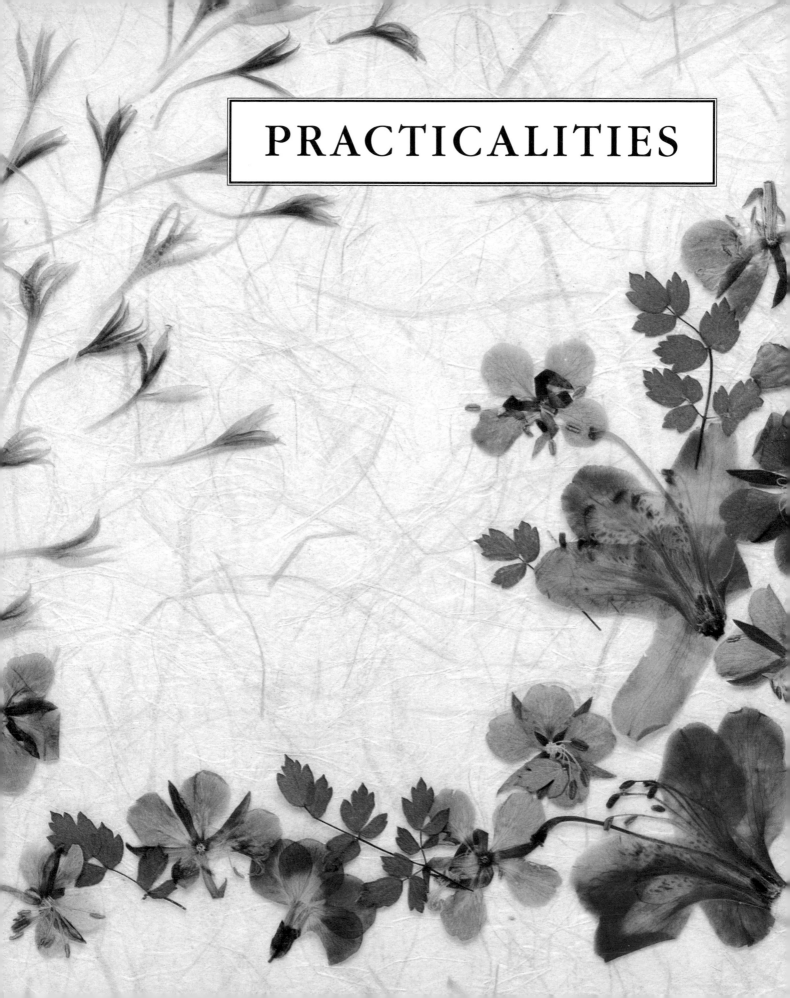

PRACTICALITIES

PRACTICALITIES

Flower-pressing is not difficult – the main personal quality that is required is a willingness to experiment. Nevertheless, there are some tips that will help to ensure success in the practical aspects of pressing and using flowers and other plant material.

Fuchsia flowers are best pressed apart from their leaves, ensuring that they do not overlap one another while drying. They can be reassembled later into flowering sprays, though not necessarily with the same components.

The first practical point to make about flower pressing is that the paper on which the flowers rest while drying must be truly absorbent. Glossy magazine paper will not work: the moisture will have nowhere to go, and the flowers are sure to rot. Blotting paper is good, but there is really no need to go to the expense of buying it, because another source of excellent paper is readily available.

Indeed, once you take up pressed-flower picture-making, you will probably never again throw away an outdated phone book. The rather thin but absorbent paper is very suitable for the purpose, and plentiful enough to be used in pads, several sheets at a time. Though absorbent, it is non-woolly, and will not therefore cling unduly to delicate petals, sepals and stamens. It can be used just as it is without the need for inserts of tissue or blotting paper, though in practice it may prove more convenient to make use of a folded sheet anyway. This way the finished product can be lifted out wholesale, ready for instant use or for transfer to a storage album.

To avoid having to pore through a thick phone book in search of the item you require, disrupting and dislodging everything else in the process, you can make a paper bookmark for each "entry". Suitably marked, a phone book makes an admirable storage place too, if not for flowers then certainly for leaves, and specifically for the larger leaves, as these are less likely to be displaced or damaged when riffling through the pages.

Folded newspapers are ideal for pressing your material, so you will find yourself saving these too. Folding each exactly down the middle will make the job much easier. You will need to interpose some tissue or blotting paper, however, as drying petals and leaves are liable to take on an imprint, and end up covered with snippets of news. Kitchen towels are not altogether suitable. They do the job very efficiently, but leave an indelible cobblestone pattern on the petals of larger flowers.

Once you have arranged your plant material within the sheets of absorbent paper, you can simply weight the layers down with heavy books or bricks and then leave them for the required time (see page 32). The longer it is left, the more colour will

With wings of purple iris petals, a body of sallow catkin and clover, eyes of sorrel, antennae of old-man's-beard, and a proboscis borrowed from a fuchsia flower, the hawk moth sips nectar while hovering over the lily bed.

be retained. You may, however, need to change the paper several times if it becomes at all damp.

What with outdated phone books, old newspapers and bricks, your basic equipment may sound somewhat primitive, but such makeshift materials will very likely prove more efficient than a ready-made flower press, which is usually fiddly in operation and all too soon filled up. One or two proper presses are useful to have around, however, particularly when you are travelling or away visiting for the weekend. They can be bought fairly cheaply, so it's really not worth trying to make one yourself, unless you are a do-it-yourself addict.

Arranging material in the press

Practise with some less important flowers at first in case you spoil them; otherwise, there should be no problems. Always press material of the same thickness in one layer, to make sure everything receives optimum pressure. When arranging material in the press, or between the pages of the outdated phone book, try to coax it into natural curves. Make it look right before drying, for it is often impossible to adjust it afterwards. Straight lines are not so useful as curving ones, though they have their place in formal designs, and even sometimes in floral scenes.

It will pay handsome dividends to take particular care with the actual pressing. Ensure that the petals lie exactly as you will want them to lie when using them in a picture. When you have a lot to press, it is tempting to throw them in any old way, but this is a temptation to be resisted. If they are not going to look right, you are wasting your time and material. Never allow them to touch one another in the press – even if they do not stick fast, the delicate petals will bear deeply impressed scars of this contact forever.

However carefully you do it, you will occasionally get material sliding about as you close the book or screw the top on the press. Despite all your care, a couple of flowers may become stuck together by the tips of their petals, or sometimes by much closer contact. Rather than risk breaking the petals by trying to separate them, and certainly if you have extra separate flowers to spare, leave them permanently attached, and use them in a design that calls for two flowers close together. You will quite often be overlapping flowers a little in your pictures anyway. They look more natural that way.

If, instead of a straight-up-and-down press, you use a folding press, a folded sheet of newspaper or the pages of a book, make sure the direction in which the pressure applies itself is appropriate for the type

Buttercups heat-pressed in profile need the stems removing as these tend to squash out of proportion. They make ideal feathers for a bird picture, in which case the calyx too is best removed along with the stem after pressing and drying.

of material being pressed. Some flowers need opening out, and others need flattening down. It is difficult to adjust dried petals which have folded themselves wrongly, so it is important to try to get them right in the first place. Sometimes a helping squash between finger and thumb will get them to lie flat in the way you want.

Larger flowers pressed full-face are normally best used without stems, which should be snipped off cleanly as close to the base of the sepals as possible. Large petals pressed so as to overlie their stems seldom look right; they will be forever corrugated.

Flowers pressed in profile are a different matter, and stems may be left on as a matter of course. Should the stems prove to be unwanted later (they sometimes squash so that they appear disproportionately broad), they can easily be nipped off when you are placing them in the picture. You will find exceptions, of course, and the rule does not really apply to the smaller flowers.

Some stems have a lineal bias and will press flat. Rosebay willowherb, for instance, can be pressed full-face with the stems attached, and no harm will be done, while tiny filler flowers such as stitchwort can be allowed to face where they will. The problem chiefly involves large and showy flowers with a single layer of smooth petal, such as pansies, pelargoniums or single roses.

Complicated or double flowers, or those with a thick central boss, are often best depetalled first and the parts pressed separately, to be reassembled later, either according to nature or according to your fancy (see page 46).

The drying process

One can never be quite sure how plant material is going to behave in the press and afterwards, as there are so many obscure factors involved. It is pretty well impossible to apply the sort of scientific control which would ensure that all your material receives a set standard of treatment, that it will have a certain moisture content, or that it has been picked at a precisely certain stage of development. Guesswork and sheer luck will have major parts to play.

The drying process may be complete in a few days when the weather is warm and dry, or if the press is kept in a dry and airy place. When the petals are small and comparatively moisture-free, particularly in the case of separated petals and small leaves, there is seldom any trouble. Other, bulkier materials may take a few months, particularly if the weather is moist.

The fact is, your material cannot become any drier than the surrounding atmosphere. So much depends upon factors that are unknown or beyond your control that it is best to look upon the whole exercise as an experiment. What proves successful this year may lead to total failure the next. There can be no hard-and-fast rules beyond your own experience and simple commonsense.

Some flowers are much more reliable than

others, but results are still bound to vary widely. For this reason, if a flower or leaf looks to you as though it may be suitable, do not reject it out of hand merely because you have read or been told that it is sure to fade, turn black or otherwise disappoint, or because you have fared badly with it before. Last year's failure may be this year's success (or vice versa).

Excessive moisture on either the inside or the outside of a plant when pressed will tend to cause it to darken. Excessive dryness at the time of picking, on the other hand, such as you might find during a drought, tends to make it fade; but even this is no hard-and-fast rule. Just try anything that is abundantly available, but be prepared for disappointments.

Atmospheric moisture is something you can do little about. If the weather is excessively damp, or if it has been raining during the night, even though your flowers may seem to have dried out and the petals may look and feel dry, the chances are that they will bear an invisible film of moisture. If they do, they will probably spoil in the press. Even normally reliable subjects such as pelargoniums and delphiniums may lose their bright colours in these circumstances; it pays to dab each flower with soft tissues before pressing them.

Heat pressing

Any highly valued flowers (or their separated petals), can be given special treatment. (This particularly applies to those which have a naturally high moisture content or a sticky nature, such as azalea, tulip and iris.) First they should be heat-pressed. This can be done quite simply with an ordinary iron (without steam), using a moderate setting suitable for silk or wool. You will need to press hard, so if your ironing board is at all flimsy, it is best done on the floor, using a pad of newspaper beneath a folded sheet of blotting paper to hold the flowers. Maintain the pressure for about half a minute.

As soon as they have cooled they should be removed from the blotter and pressed again in tissue paper sheathed with newspapers. This should safeguard against any propensity to stick, and remove the threat

Rosebay willowherb flowers are easy to press with or without their stems. After pressing they tend to fade very gradually changing from deep carmine to pale mauve. In this design, the flowers have been provided with the leafy young trailing tips of old-man's-beard.

of discoloration. When you have hundreds of flowers to press, this double routine can prove a little tedious, but it is the best policy every time if you have only a few choice flowers to see to.

Petals that tend towards transparency have this tendency greatly increased by heat pressing. Far from being a drawback, transparency often greatly enhances the appearance of a pressed-flower. Wood anemones, for instance, brown slightly when they are cold-pressed, but when pressed with heat they stay clear white and translucent (though they will then need a very light background in order to be seen at their best).

Yellow flowers, in particular, such as celandine, yellow loosestrife and marigold, if not completely transparent like amber when pressed with heat, take on a certain translucency while retaining their clear yellow colour, at least for a time. (Some, like forsythia and creeping Jenny, become fairly translucent even when pressed cold in the normal way.) They look beautiful against any background light enough to reflect, but tend to disappear against a black background or any other dark colour. Unlike celandines, buttercups darken with heat, and in any case they are less liable than celandines to fade when they are pressed full face.

Because the most natural-looking appearance may often be attained in a picture by overlapping your flowers slightly here and there, the question of transparency should be borne in mind if heat is to be used. It seldom looks right when you are able to see the overlapped parts of neighbouring flowers through the petals, so it is as well to ensure that those with a tendency to become transparent should lie

beneath the opaque ones – that is, they should be fixed in place first. Better still, if you can match damaged petal edges or leaves one to another, the overlapping process will be quite painlessly achieved in all cases, with no wastage whatsoever.

Between the sheets
Unless you have a vast array of material (in which case you will need to construct a system of racks or well-aired shelves), a convenient way to store pressed-flowers ready for use is in a photograph album that has transparent sheets. When you use this method, however, be sure to include a sheet of absorbent paper for the flowers to rest on between the sheets, because they are sure to contain some residual moisture, and this is liable to start some kind of reaction that will allow deterioration to set in. A simple insert of ordinary white bond paper, which can be replaced at intervals, is all that is required.

Fading and colour changes
You will find that flowers are individuals where pressing is concerned, but there are certain general characteristics which remain

Autumn leaves need only the minimum of pressing but they should be stored flat. They should never be pressed with heat, as this may turn the shades of red and yellow to a dull, flat brown.

Opposite *Buttercups pressed with heat produce a range of tawny orange shades, and become translucent – ideal for the plumage of a brown owl! Use darker flowers for the edge and shaded areas, lighter ones for the highlights. Ox-eye daisies provide the eyes, using more than one layer of petals. The feathered feet are sweet william petals, while the beak is an alstroemeria tip.*

Blue flowers usually fade, but trailing lobelia is an exception to the rule, as both the flowers and the foliage usually darken with age. The larkspur foliage at the base will gradually fade to near straw colour.

fairly constant, even when applied to entire plant families. Flowers of the pea family, for instance, are not as a rule very good pressers (though again there are exceptions). Sweet peas, in particular, are rather hopeless subjects for pressing. Not only are they moist and flimsy, but the discoloration that immediately sets in rarely lends itself to artistic recuperation – though there is always room for experimentation.

In general, flowers that are in pure, bright colours, especially yellow, will keep their colour longer than pastel or subtly shaded flowers. Creams can become brownish, while blues may fade a little.

Some flowers darken with age. Broom flowers, although so typical of dry places, are full of moisture, and almost invariably darken from the edges. But these dark-rimmed petals still retain a glowing central zone of treacly amber which can often find a suitable place in your picture.

Gorse flowers are comparatively dry, though the petals look very similar to broom, and they merely modify their clear yellow to an overall amber, or the muted ochre of crystallized honey. Gorse flowers, incidentally, unlike the others, can only be picked separately (and with caution), removing them from the tips of their prickly shoots. They look rather more like separate petals than whole flowers, and this fact offers a clue as to their best use: they have been arranged to represent the petals of many an exotic flower which grew only in the pressed-flower artist's imagination. They can prove a useful stopgap in another way too. Apart from their main spring flowering season, individual gorse blossoms, like the ubiquitous dandelion, may be found in flower during every month, and probably on every day of the year.

Laburnum flowers usually behave very well, and though they may fade sooner or later, they will fade to sheer white, which some say is every bit as attractive as their original yellow.

If you wish to enhance the colours by tinting the petals, use a water soluble felt-tipped pen, spreading the colour evenly with a damp cotton bud (Q-Tip) or your finger. You may well come to the opinion that it is the emerging colour which deserves enhancing, rather than the departing one. You will make sure then that the new-look white flowers are pure white rather than grubby grey.

Gentle persuasion

Some flowers start to curl up soon after they have been picked, and need gentle titivation with a paintbrush or a fingertip to persuade them to press flat. Wild flowers are more prone to do this than are garden flowers. The petals of bell-shaped flowers often crumple in this way, and they can appear completely shapeless by the time you get them to the press. However, such a flower can sometimes be persuaded to bell out again as good as new if you blow gently into the cup. The petals will fill out like sails in the breeze. It will probably be necessary to trap a petal tip between thumb and forefinger first, to provide a stable base. The flower can then be pressed truly flat. You will find this valuable in the case of the more floppy campanulas, such as harebell; the common and musk mallows, which often close up after picking; the herbaceous garden geraniums and the meadow cranesbill.

Pressed flowers that stick to the pressing paper can usually be loosened by passing your hand beneath the sheet and gently bending it to and fro beneath the stuck petals. With fragile flowers that break if you lift them indiscriminately, a slim knife blade slipped underneath will often do the trick, provided you can first loosen a petal tip. Once a petal has been raised, however, thumb and forefinger will usually do the rest. Some flower pressers like to use sharp-pointed tweezers, but everyone will develop the method best suited to themselves.

Tiny flowers that drop before you can get them to the press can be a real problem. Both germander speedwell and, in particular, the common speedwell have a habit of doing this. Usually the entire

Flimsy-petalled flowers such as leopard's-bane, some others such as aubrieta, fine foliage such as tufted vetch, and tiny plants such as stitchwort all tend to roll up if pasted directly. The backing paper should be lightly pasted first and your material then arranged carefully in place.

flower comes off in the press, and sticks fast to the pressing paper. You may be able to prevent this from happening by sticking fresh flowers of this type directly onto the backing card and allowing them to dry there, pressed *in situ*. It is worth an experiment, at any rate.

All pressed material needs to be stuck (at least partially) onto the backing paper or board. For leaves and solid flowers that will not readily crumple or crumble,

Silverweed is robust enough to forgive any mistake you might make when pasting, but it is almost impossible to adjust the bell flowers of campanula, or a clematis seedhead, once they have been touched with glue.

a spot of glue may be applied to the back of the flower itself with a fine paintbrush. For more fragile sorts, there are very useful roll-on paper-glue dispensers that enable you to place a thin patch of adhesive over the correct spot in your picture, then arrange the petals carefully in place. The glue usually dries invisibly, but if it doesn't, any smeary gloss effect will tend to disappear when you cover the finished picture with protective glass or clear plastic film.

There will inevitably be the occasional casualty. Dried flowers will sometimes shatter, and many of the larger or bulkier types of flower cannot conveniently be pressed whole. But when you arrange your picture, a speck of glue will enable you to reposition any shed petals or parts. Any clear glue or paper paste will do the job, and you will probably find a type that suits you best.

Spare-part bank

You will find it a good idea, and increasingly necessary, to keep a spare-part bank or hospital bay of floral transplant organs. This can include odd petals or central "disc floret" sections of chrysanthemums or marigolds, tulip petals – flowers broken beyond repair but which perhaps may be used to patch others. They can often save the day and brighten up the ailing flower picture.

Sources of plant material

Your own garden is likely to be your first source of supply for plant material. Your second source will probably be the gardens of relatives and friends too polite to say no. But flower sellers' stalls and barrows are useful as well and need not be too expensive – a little goes a long way for the pressed-flower artist.

Of course, commonsense is called for when picking any flower growing elsewhere than in your garden. Land, as a rule, is owned by someone, and there are legal requirements. A simple request may well reap great benefits, but those road-verge flowers due to be beheaded by a tractor-drawn mower may and should be harvested when you get the chance. If you do use wild plants, and even if you are exceptionally greedy as you hunt along road verge and field edge, you will probably pick less in a season than any hungry cow would eat in five minutes.

Nevertheless, you should never pick or dig up any protected plants. (Lists of these are available from local libraries, natural history societies and some wild-flower guidebooks.) Also, certain fragile or unusual sites are completely protected, so that it is illegal to either pick or dig up even common plants there.

If you come across a wild flower that is the only one of its kind in the vicinity, do not pick it. Similarly, if you are picking flowers at the seed stage, shake some seeds onto the ground. Always leave behind some flowers of the kind you have picked.

Many of the plants which are widespread in temperate zones throughout much of the world – like the ferns – are among the most useful for the pressed-flower artist. Tiny sprigs are all you need; you don't have to uproot the plant. You don't even really need to know which fern is which – if it is common in your area, try it, and if it works for you, use it.

Centre of attention
Blind or blank-looking flowers, such as phlox or mophead hydrangea florets, or even a circlet of leaves such as those provided by the woodruff, can be livened up with the addition of a centrepiece. Some stamens from a hypericum, a small lawn daisy or merely a solitary flower from elder or pyracantha are admirable for this. Your ingenuity will add a new interest and bring what might have been a rather dull flower to life.

Greenery
In spring and summer, greenery is so abundant that there is always the temptation

Light and shade can be expressed by using a black or very dark-coloured backing board, with a few fairly large light-coloured flowers in the centre. This picture features two kinds of rose, larkspur, mallow, potentilla, meadowsweet and a few hydrangea florets, surrounded by trailing tips of bindweed which seem to disappear into the background.

Pick small sprigs of goat-willow leaves in the spring, while they are still young and pliable. Those at the ends of the twigs are best, and picking these will encourage leaf buds to grow quickly and replace them. These sprigs with stems attached are easy to arrange naturally in your picture.

to leave your leafy requirements until it is too late. Usable new leaves are not always as easy to come by as you might imagine. By high summer those that would otherwise have been suitable, such as the hedgerow hawthorn, hazel and field maple, if not too large, have grown too tough and woody to make a good job. It is also possible to overlook the need for greenery altogether in the search for suitable flowers – so make the most of a supply of good leaves while you can. Later on may just be too late.

One of the nicest leaves to include in the scenic type of picture is probably sallow or goat willow, as the sprigs lend themselves so admirably well to the task, and look so natural. As with most trees, they are liable to become quite ragged with the holes eaten in them by insects; in some years this will be worse than in others. But unless the

damage is very severe, this scarcely detracts from their beauty after pressing, and certainly not from their natural appearance. They have a habit of curling slightly along the margins so as to show the contrast of woolly grey undersurface and dark green upperside, and this lends a wonderfully storm-tossed look to a leaf picture.

Almost any slender stem can, of course, be kept in case of need, even if not wanted for its leaves or flowers. Grass stems too can serve as flower stems in stiffly formal bunches. Ivy-leaved toadflax is rather too fine in the stem, with its "thick" and "thin" ends comparatively undefined, and the leaves too few and far between and often of the wrong scale. A well-balanced spray of ivy-leaved toadflax is a valuable find.

Tendrils, tips and trails

Always keep your eyes open for the more transient things. In very early spring you may have a lucky find: tiny ivy leaves clinging closely to the bark of some old oak tree, tinted pink and pale green, the veins ivory or cream against the primrose yellow of the leaf. These are a prize for the pressed-flower artist. Ordinary mature ivy leaves are not so delicately beautiful, though they are still useful. Ivy is the unmistakable symbol of friendship and faithfulness and makes a wonderfully evocative addition to the decorated letter or greetings card sent to an old friend, long absent but not forgotten.

This seasonal type of ivy-leaf variegation is more transient than that of the fixed cultivars such as Gold Heart or Glacier. Heat should not be used when pressing them or they will immediately darken and look like any other ivy leaf. They should be allowed to dry in their own

The luxuriant growth of a wild-flower meadow is suggested by this simple but well-balanced arrangement. The flowers include cornflower, reassembled without the hard heads, leopard's-bane and a solitary bird's-foot trefoil, with grass, a spike of sorrel and leaves of tufted vetch.

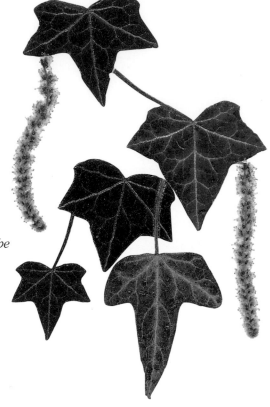

Young ivy leaves, with their distinctive shape, often show a delicate combination of colours in the spring. They are simplicity itself to press and store. Interest can be added by combining them with "catkins" of goatsbeard.

time, and they will quickly do this without any special pressing routine – simply slip them between folded sheets of newspaper. Once dried, however, these pretty little leaves can be subjected to heat, or over-laminated, without altering their delicate colours.

Ivy climbs without the aid of tendrils, but many tendrilled leaves, tips and trails can become effective components of a picture. Be sure, therefore, not to miss an opportunity to collect a good supply. It is so easy to put it off – leaves and trails never seem so urgent a matter as seasonal flowers. But they too have a comparatively short season, and soon go past their best. The trails of ivy itself, Boston ivy, Virginia creeper and many clematises often prove too thick and heavy to be of much use. Bryony, too, is coarse, though usually thinner than these.

In the countryside, bindweed, or convolvulus, is one of the most conspicuous of trailing plants. The flowers are to be admired as they scramble over hedges and sprawl along the verge, but they are seldom worth the trouble of pressing, as they are unlikely to give good results. Best is the small, pinkish-flowered field bindweed, which is very widespread and tends to sprawl along the grass verges of lanes rather than climb hedges like its larger relative. The flowers, though their texture remains satiny, become hopelessly shapeless, but you don't need the flowers. You don't need long trails of leafy stems either, but what you *do* need are the twining tips – the top few inches of every shoot. If you start picking these very early in the season, bindweed can be harvested over and over. Twining tips and sprigs, together with the tiniest leaves, add marvellous finishing touches to floral scenes and bouquets. They are perfect ivy substitutes to climb up miniature Japanese veneer trees, and they are useful in abstract designs too. The leaves usually darken with age, but they remain shapely and attractive.

Bindweed often binds around itself in a double twisting trail which, provided the leaves are small enough, can look very effective. It is best to arrange your trails as you want them, before they are too dry to bend. But it doesn't always work like this, and it is as well to remember that twining stems and trailers which have stiffened in the wrong direction can be coaxed back into the shape you want. To do this, press them under padding, briefly, with a hot iron. A few seconds of this treatment should render them pliable enough to be rearranged into suitable curves.

The twining theme is a good bet for an effective picture when other inspiration is lacking, as it looks picturesque. However, it does make solid, straight stems seem

ungainly and superfluous. When making arrangements and hanging sprays which twine, in fact, there is often no need to provide a supporting or linking stem at all. While a free-standing flower arrangement naturally cannot stand without supporting stems, you are not bound by any such restriction, and each flower or leaf can follow another quite naturally without actually having to link up. Even if you leave a gap between them, it will not look odd, provided their positioning is logical. The viewer's aesthetic eye effectively fills in the gaps.

Mixing and matching

Many flowers that look delicately beautiful when growing and entire, like the yellow snapdragon-heads of toadflax, squash sadly into a shapeless mess if pressed indiscriminately. For the larger flowers that behave like this, it may be better to dissect them and press the parts

Any trailing tips can be added to change and soften the character of stiff spikes such as agrimony. The celandine flowers at their base look natural without the need for anchoring stems.

separately. By mingling petals and parts from different flowers, and leaves and flowers from different plants, you will be making up new flowers and new plants in a way that a botanist, or a dedicated botanical artist, would probably find shocking. But this is your own freestyle impressionism, and it is particularly satisfying to have produced a beautiful picture with exquisite flowers, none of which actually exists in nature, and which owe their beauty both to nature's art and to your own skill.

Good "mixing" flowers are always valuable – lawn daisies, for instance. Larger flowers of the daisy type, such as ox-eye, are seldom heavily petalled enough to overlap other material without the latter showing through. Lawn daisies, however,

Left Flowers, seedheads, or even leaves which may look too plain or uninteresting on their own may often be combined with a different, smaller flower to produce an exotic bloom out of your own imagination, with or without the addition of artificial colour. Here cottongrass is centred with hawkbit.

With its flimsy petals, the common lawn daisy does little to conceal underlying flowers or leaves but it can transform a dull subject into an original creation.

are ideal, not because their petals are suitable for concealing anything, but because of their dainty size and shape. They are exactly right for superimposing on other flowers that have faded or are just too plain for use by themselves. Many unpromising subjects can be perked up with full-face daisies, and still remain convincing as flowers in their own right. They make convincing centres too for large flowers (such as shrubby hybrid hypericums) which happen to have lost their stamens. Used on their own, lawn daisies are perhaps at their most charming when featured, not in scenes, but on little gift objects, bookmarks, cards and other trivia.

Lawn daisies may be pressed full-face (almost always the best way), in profile or half-profile. But even if needed only in profile, they should be picked when fully open on a sunny day, and pressed immediately after picking, otherwise they are liable to close up in protest, and cannot then be persuaded to open. Full-face daisies are usually best without stems, and though they are normally left on when

pressed in profile, they sometimes flatten out of proportion and look unsightly. Single daisies with pink-tinged petals are the most ornamental; double garden varieties do not press well and usually end up mildewed and blackened.

Damage limitation

Once you start looking at flowers with a view to pressing them, you will realize just how rare it is to find perfection. The majority of blooms, large or small, are slightly damaged or flawed in some way. There are so many creatures and organisms that feed on them, and the weather does a fair amount of damage as well. As already mentioned, damaged petals can be concealed quite easily by overlapping them with other, sound flowers. In large pictures, dozens of damaged flowers may be successfully camouflaged in this way, and the same principle, of course, applies to leaves. Blemishes can disappear as if by magic while the natural appearance of your picture grows.

If things have gone too far and the petals of your pressed-flowers are really ruined and about to be thrown away, don't forget the sepals. Flowers often have ornamental centrepieces which are normally hidden by petals and stamens. Pelargoniums, for instance, have dainty little green stars which can be used even if the petals have to be scrapped.

In the press, large petals very readily pick up an indelible impression of lumpy pressing materials – such as cardboard with a corrugated interior or patterned kitchen towels – so that they come out speckled, mottled or chequered rather like a fritillary flower. The result, though obviously unintended, is not necessarily unsightly. It can

The repetitive pattern of pink and purple sprays of larkspur with rose leaves is given fluidity by the lacy yellow circles of fennel flowers, which add a touch of colourful gaiety to what might otherwise have seemed an unadventurous design.

give your larger flowers the appearance of damask or brocade, and look quite attractive. If you have several which have suffered this fate, you might save them all for a fritillary-chequered picture on a crimpy silklike backing, which could look very effective.

As mentioned previously, undamaged but over-bulky flowers will often need to be broken up carefully into their component parts before pressing, then either reassembled or reconstructed into entirely new flowers of your own invention. Surprisingly, perhaps, it is usually more difficult to reassemble them into convincing representations of their former selves. In any event, you need to make sure when rearranging long-petalled composites such as marigolds that each petal appears to radiate directly from the exact centre, like the rays of the sun. Particularly in the case of flimsy petals, it is often best to glue the paper rather than the petals; fix the centre in place, then, grasping each petal in turn by the tip, draw it across the centre point so as to align it exactly.

Large monocots, such as daffodils, alstroemerias, lilies and irises, require a different approach. Daffodils and lilylike flowers may be pressed whole, though the leaves are usually best split. The larger irises, being of more complicated structure, will need their flowers to be depetalled; the leaves and the flower sheaths may be split up the middle before pressing. The sheaths will still curl picturesquely, but will be easier to handle and, of course, double in number. One is sometimes recommended to split trumpet flowers such as daffodils, lilies and rhododendrons, to reduce their bulk (and double the stock). By all means try this, but unless they are to be reassembled later, it means that the all-important third dimensional effect is lost, and your picture could look flat and uninspiring.

Camouflaging and contouring

Depending on the nature of your picture, unless it is one with no stems at all, you may frequently find that you have too many minor stems and loose ends on view. Sooner or later the vexed question will arise: what do you do with the bases of small clumps and single flowers? Should you leave them apparently floating in mid-air, or conceal them with another clump, or flower, so that the problem repeats itself lower down? Too much of this can lead to a hopelessly cluttered picture. To adopt the opposite extreme and leave everything unconnected will overstrain the aesthetic eye, and cause your miniature scene to lack that air of solid reality that would have completed the illusion.

One answer is to use a tiny sprig of moss as camouflage. Longer trails of moss can also be used to sketch in the foreground and suggest contours. For contour use it is best to use different kinds and colours of moss to represent foreground and background respectively. The smaller-leaved and lighter-coloured kinds can represent distance, and the coarser, larger-sprigged mosses and brighter greens can be placed in the foreground.

If your flower sprigs are selected according to size as well, with the largest in the front and the smallest at the back, the effect can be stunningly realistic and your picture will be full of life.

Stitchwort is a typical landscaping sprig which can be used to manipulate horizons. But never assume that because they are abundant, and because the flowers are so tiny, they can be thrown into the press any old way. Every sprig should be arranged with care, even though the flowers themselves will have to be pressed more or less as they come, owing to their size. Having very little bulk, they will press quite flat without squashing, but it is up to you to ensure that they lie on the pressing paper in a naturally picturesque manner, without bunching, otherwise the effect you are after will be lost.

This flamboyant collection of flowers demonstrates the rainbow range of natural colours available. The foliage includes ivy, spurge and birch.

*This plain, upright vase
and smoothly rounded
group of flowers are reminiscent of a flower painting by Renoir. The flowers
are chrysanthemum,
larkspur and phlox. The
finished picture has been
laminated, and this
enables a few smudges of
glass paint to be added to
make a solid table top,
and give an "impression"
of the painter's style.*

Laminating and mounting

It is a debatable point, but many people believe that a completed picture needs a transparent, close-fitting cover to protect it, to exclude air as far as possible, prevent undue curling of petals and leaves, and generally improve the overall appearance.

Glass pressed flat, of course, will do the trick (though it is not really airtight), but doing this precludes the use of a cut mount, except for the thinnest paper kinds, which do not look so good.

A thick, well-cut mount does greatly improve many pictures, good and mediocre

alike, adding all-important depth, so it is worth going to the extra trouble of providing one when you feel that the picture merits the attention.

Certainly you will need a mount when the base or edges of the picture display the loose, unwanted woody ends of twigs, because the mount will hide them from view. A thick mount used with uncovered pressed flowers allows the material to wrinkle and shrink out of shape, which is another good reason for covering the completed picture with a thin laminate of plastic.

When PVC laminating film is used with a hot iron (or, better still, with a hot press), a non-glare surface is needed in order to avoid giving the picture a rather plasticky appearance. This surface is quite easily achieved – simply place a plastic sponge sheet, or a piece of coarse fabric, between the laminating film and the heat source, so that a slightly variable and therefore anti-reflective surface is imprinted onto the laminate.

Glossing over it

Even dull, lifeless-looking material can be brought miraculously to life by laminating, or the addition of any transparent, semi-glossy, self-sealing cover. Old and unpromising-looking leaves, wrinkled after many years of storage, need never be discarded. They will be positively rejuvenated by lamination. The heat working on atmospheric moisture, the firm pressure, and the smooth semi-glossy surface which results will really make them look alive.

As already mentioned, an old and faded picture can often be given a new lease of life by sticking newly pressed material on top of the old, to add fresh colour and bestow an attractive double-petalled effect. A cosmetic rescue operation of this sort need not be ruled out simply because you have laminated or plastic-covered the original. Simply fix your fresh material on top of the film and then, if you want to, apply a second seal, or relaminate.

If you do this, however, make sure that the new material is truly dry first. In the case of the first batch, residual moisture could always escape gradually through the backing card, but now it will be trapped, and this could well cause trouble. If you heat-laminate (and a laminating press exerts considerable pressure) it is a wise precaution to pinprick the film well before applying it, to allow moisture to escape during the few seconds before the heat finally seals up the holes.

Small leaves such as these on the young trailing tips of old-man's-beard are easily damaged, and small flowers such as forget-me-nots readily drop their petals. A protective film or heat-lamination permanently protects them from both wear-and-tear and atmospheric change.

PROJECTS

MIDSUMMER SCENE

In this fanciful scene, a solitary leopard's-bane flower plays the role of setting sun, reflecting golden light onto the drift of pansies below, and the overhanging sprays of goat willow and sprigs of Russian vine. The picture is made on a canvas panel which was first given a light colour wash.

Picture size
355 x 456mm (14 x 18in)

You will need
Coarse-grained canvas panel
Acrylic or oil paints in sap green, chrome yellow with titanium white, and cobalt violet
Paintbrush, size 10 (1.2cm or ½in)
PVA (white) glue
Small paintbrush
Tweezers

Plant material
1 *Leopard's-bane*
2 *Impatiens "Firelake" leaves*
3 *Goat-willow leaves*
4 *Russian-vine catkins*
5 *Pansies*
6 *Pelargoniums*

1 Give the canvas panel a light wash of colour, using chrome yellow with white for the centre circle, sap green around the edges of the top half and cobalt violet around the edges of the bottom half. Blend the colours where they meet, to avoid hard edges. If you are using acrylics, the paint will dry quickly. If you are using oils, put the panel away for a week or so to dry before proceeding.

2 Glue the leopard's-bane flower towards the centre to represent the sun. This will then be the point of reference for all your other material.

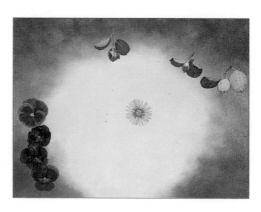

3 Place the goat-willow leaves around the upper part of the picture, commencing with the lowest leaves, reflexed slightly towards the sun. Start placing the darker pansies at the bottom of the picture towards the picture edges (*bottom of previous column*).

4 Build up the foliage progressively, so that the stem ends of each sprig are concealed beneath the leaves. Try to obtain the natural appearance of wind-tossed foliage as you work upwards towards the top of the panel.

5 Add the remaining outermost pansies, overlapping them as necessary to best advantage (*below*).

6 Fill in towards the centre with the lighter-coloured pansies and the pelargoniums.

7 Now add the impatiens leaves and the Russian vine catkins. As always, position this extra plant material loosely at first, making absolutely certain that the picture as a whole is well balanced before sticking them all down.

TREE AT THE WATERSIDE

A black backing board lends drama to this picture. A lake, drawn with pastel crayons, and a tree cut out of wood veneer-faced paper and outlined with mossy green pastel, form a basic structure around which the plant material is arranged.

Picture size
400 x 300mm (15¾ x 11¾in)

You will need
Black backing board
Japanese wood veneer-faced paper
Pastel crayon in blue-grey, moss green, and black
Pastel crayon in white (if using a silver veneer) or in pale brown or orange (if using a brown veneer)
Tweezers
Ruler, craft knife
PVA (white) glue
Small paintbrush

Plant material
1 Buddleia leaves
2 Lady's bedstraw
3 Elder flowers
4 Reindeer moss
5 Tufted vetch leaves
6 Lunaria (honesty) flower
7 Rosebay willowherb flowers
8 Bird's-foot trefoil flowers
9 Heuchera flowers
10 Moss
11 Fern

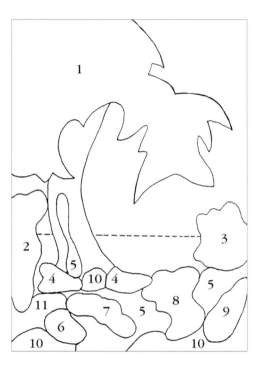

At the base of the tree is an interesting clump of grey-white reindeer moss, a type of lichen. The leaves dropping over the water are not really weeping willow (though these might do as well) but buddleia, demonstrating the contrast between upper and lower surfaces. The flowers are rosebay willowherb with a solitary lunaria in front to give them foreground and depth, bird's-foot trefoil and heuchera. The bushes on either side are lady's bedstraw and elder, while trails of tufted vetch fill in the ground-cover and sprawl up the tree.

1 Draw the lake, a third of the way up your backing board, using a ruler and the flat side of a blue-grey pastel crayon. Add touches of white wave tops with a white pastel crayon, smearing it gently from side to side.

2 Using a craft knife, cut out a tree from the veneer and glue it onto the backing board (*below*).

3 Use moss green pastel around the edges of the veneer tree to give it solidity. Add a touch of black pastel to represent root buttresses and, if you like, a hole higher up the tree. Outline these black areas with the green pastel.

4 Apply highlights very sparingly to the tree with white, pale brown or orange pastel, smearing it gently in the direction of the tree's growth.

5 Place the moss and reindeer moss at the base of the tree. Start positioning the buddleia leaves for the tree foliage, commencing with the lower leaves and

overlapping slightly as you proceed (*right*). The topmost leaves will have only their tips showing in the picture.

6 If you wish, use tufted vetch leaves to create a creeper to climb the trunk.

7 Add the ground vegetation, with a clump at each side rising above the horizon – that is, above the line of the lake. Try to avoid cluttering the foreground. The trailing leaves of tufted vetch effectively cover the area without appearing too solid.

KINGFISHER

Poised on its mossy stump, this kingfisher stands out in sharp focus against a soft aquatic background. A variety of blue petals and small flowers make up the bird's plumage, contrasting brilliantly with the orange flag iris petals of its breast.

Picture size
280 x 200mm (11 x 8in)

You will need
Heavy watercolour paper
Pen or pencil
Pastel crayons in moss green, dark brown and white
Pastel crayons in blue, orange and brown (optional)
PVA (white) glue
Small paintbrush
Tweezers

Plant material
1 Blue petals and small flowers: delphinium, larkspur, speedwell, forget-me-not, lobelia
2 Flag iris petals
3 Alstroemeria petal (folded)
4 Ox-eye daisy petals
5 Pelargonium petal (folded)
6 Ox-eye daisy (stripped centre)
7 Moss

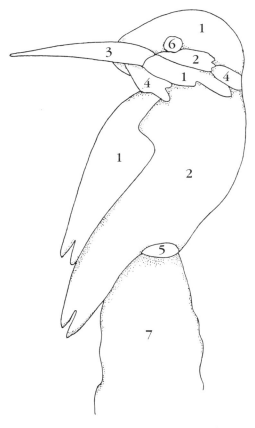

When making a pressed-flower picture of a bird or animal, particularly when it is intended as a fairly accurate representation rather than a caricature, always try to use the natural sweep of the petals and the direction of the veins to emphasize the curving outline of the creature you are depicting. Sweeping lines create the illusion of movement, and without them the subject is apt to look either dumpy or wooden. It lends plump solidity to the subject when these streaks and veins, following the curve of the back or breast, seem to mould themselves to the natural shape and pattern of the creature.

In this example, the dark veins of the

brightly coloured flag iris petals provide the long, gracefully rounded curves and feathered pattern of the kingfisher's chestnut-orange breast. The natural sequence of lighter and darker striations adds to the illusion of feathers in dappled, moving shade.

The wings, back and head are composed of several blue flowers. Small, separated larkspur and delphinium petals are used for the deepest royal blue and several other dark shades, while lighter highlights are provided by germander speedwell, lobelia, and a forget-me-not or two.

White touches at the cheek and nape are layers of ox-eye daisy petals. The centre of this flower, with sepals and "disc florets" removed, forms the eye, which is brought to life with the merest fleck of white. The foot is a pink pelargonium petal. The great dagger of a beak was formed by a single alstroemeria petal induced to fold itself along the central vein.

The mossy stump adds to the solidity of the picture. The rather blurred background was put in first, using finger-smeared pastel. The effect is to make the plumage stand out with the three-dimensional effect that a camera produces when the background is out of focus.

You will need some kind of starting guide for this type of picture, if your bird is not to look a shapeless jumble. You could lightly outline the shape with pencil and shade in the darker parts. Alternatively, you could lightly colour the broad masses, noting especially where bold strokes are needed – the wing flight feathers, for instance. Remember that you will need to stick flimsy petals on top of this colour layer, so this rules out very waxy crayon or too

Hints

• Be guided by your flower material, if you decide to make this or a different bird picture of your own design. You may have separate petals or small flowers of a predominant colour which will suggest a suitable bird subject: buttercup, celandine, and creeping Jenny, for instance, would make a beautiful canary bird.

• Even petals which have gone brown could be put to good use, with many possible subjects ranging from sparrows to eagles. Additional flowers which have retained their colour could also be incorporated to bring the browns to life. Imagine a brown speckled thrush perched amid the bright flowering sprays of spring.

dusty chalk or pastel, which will not take the glue. Pastel crayons will work best.

When selecting material, it is mainly a matter of marshalling resources and trying a piece of this and that until you achieve the effect you want. It is an excellent way to use up odd brightly coloured petals and broken flowers.

1 Draw or trace the kingfisher. If desired, lightly crayon in the colours of the kingfisher as a guide. Do the background with soft pastels in moss green, dark brown and white, smeared with the finger (*below*). The intention is to represent a brook overhung with leafy alders, the light shining through here and there and reflecting on the water.

2 Start sticking on the bird's feathers, working from the wing tips and tail end

upwards (*below*), and from the nape of the neck forwards, so as to make the petals overlap like real feathers. The blue wings should slightly overlap the orange breast.

3 Carefully fold the alstroemeria petal along the central vein to form the long, sharp beak. Take time to make it look just right.

4 Leave the mossy perch and the foot till last, folding the pink pelargonium petal in half to form the foot.

5 Finally, make the eye. The central disc of an ox-eye daisy is naturally black after the tiny florets have been removed, but it may need enhancing with a touch of black crayon, followed by a speck of white crayon to give it life.

SHADES OF BROWN AND CREAM

Inspired by seventeenth- and eighteenth-century wood carvings, these two attractive panels demonstrate that ideas for designs are to be found even in the unlikeliest of places. They also prove that flowers in shades of brown can be used to very good effect.

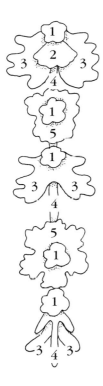

Picture size (each)
300 x 180mm (11¾ x 7in)

You will need
Sawn and polished wood, or standard-thickness veneer, or Japanese wood veneer-faced paper
Ruler
Craft knife
PVA (white) glue
Small paintbrush
Tweezers

Plant material
1 Hawthorn blossom
2 Dogwood blossom
3 Honeysuckle buds
4 Goatsbeard catkin
5 Lilac blossom
6 Hypericum calyx
7 Rose

Pressed flowers do not always keep their colour. A good way to use flowers that have turned brown is to make an exclusively brown design with a motif inspired by wood carvings, on a backing of real wood or veneer. During the seventeenth and eighteenth centuries, ornately carved wood panels were obligatory features of British stately homes. It became the practice to overlay a plain panel with carvings of a different wood with contrasting colour and grain. A noted architectural artist in this field was Grinling Gibbons, who preferred to use lime over oak. The pendant design on the darker panel was prompted by his work. The flowers used here are hawthorn, dogwood blossom, honeysuckle buds, goatsbeard catkins, and lilac.

The lighter-coloured veneer illustrates the French style. The design was suggested by panelling in Marie Antoinette's boudoir.

Like the darker panel, this design makes use of honeysuckle buds. The central flower is a double rose, surrounded by clusters of double lilacs, each centred with the woody calyx of a large-flowered hypericum. More hypericum calyces decorate the corners, their slightly greenish tinge adding interest to the design.

You can use a piece of sawn and polished wood, or a full thickness veneer, or as in this case a gossamer-thin Japanese veneer mounted on paper. The last option is easy to handle, but it is advisable to mount it on cardboard to avoid accidental creasing.

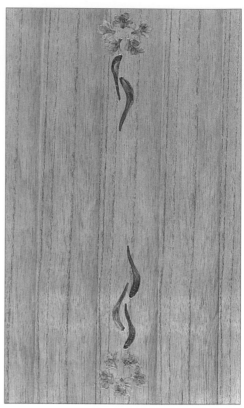

Hints
• *As an alternative to wood panels, you could use veneer paper to form the surrounding mount for a light and colourful pressed flower picture, placing brown "wood-carving" flowers and leaves to contrast with and accentuate the colours in the picture.*
• *It could also be used to frame a wedding photograph. Individual bells of campanula or wild hyacinth, or the perfectly formed tiny bells of lily-of-the-valley, which often turn an attractive shade of amber-brown when pressed, could make a series of miniature wedding bells arranged in pairs, perhaps with a bow of cyclamen or witch hazel petal.*

For either design, use a ruler to make sure you follow a straight, central, vertical line – but do not make any kind of mark on the veneer itself.

Arrange all the flowers to your complete satisfaction before gluing them down, as symmetry is all-important. It is best not to overcrowd this type of picture: simplicity is the keynote here.

Darker panel
1 If you want to make the design look like a continuous carving, position the honeysuckle buds and goatsbeard catkins first (*above*), so that their ends can be concealed beneath the flowers. Place the dogwood blossom on top of the uppermost cluster.

2 Between these, arrange the clusters of lilac blossoms. Place them far enough apart to make room for the central feature of each cluster – the hawthorn blossom. You will probably have a different selection of brown but shapely

material to be used up, but the same principles apply.

Lighter panel
1 Position the lilac blossom and honeysuckle buds at the top and bottom of the panel, leaving enough room in the centre of each cluster of lilac blossoms for the hypericum calyces (*above*).

2 Arrange another group of honeysuckle buds and lilac blossom in the centre, at right angles to the others, once again leaving room for the hypericum calyces. Add honeysuckle buds top and bottom running the same direction as those in the centre.

3 Place a hypericum calyx in the centre of each cluster of lilac blossom, and at the top and bottom outer corners near the honeysuckle buds.

4 Finish with a double rose at the centre of the arrangement.

INDIAN CARPET

The model for this picture is a distinctive type of carpet pattern dating from around 1600, and exclusive to India. The flowers portrayed in carpets of this type and period are more realistic than those featured in antique Persian carpets.

Picture size
254 x 178mm (10 x 7in)

You will need
Canvas panel
Oil or acrylic paint in
  alizarin crimson
Paintbrush, size 10
  (1.2cm or ½in)
Pencil, carbon paper
  (optional)
PVA (white) glue
Small paintbrush

Plant material
1 Heuchera
2 Pink yarrow
3 Rosebay willowherb
4 Gorse
5 Yellow alyssum
6 Fleabane
7 White clover
8 Daisy
9 Annual phlox
10 Elder
11 Moss

Given mossy stems, the small flowers used in this picture are set out individually in separate ogee compartments marked out with continuous lines of elder flowers. (The ogee, which could be described as two continuous S-shaped curves, with one the mirror image of the other, is a traditional shape that is used in carpet and textile designs, and is of Islamic origin.)

1 Paint the canvas panel and leave it to dry completely. Now lightly pencil in the ogee compartments. They need to be done very carefully and evenly if the finished picture is to look convincing. It will probably be easier to perfect the curves on a separate piece of paper the same size as the canvas panel, and then transfer the pattern onto the painted surface using carbon paper.

2 Brush glue along the ogee curves a few centimetres (an inch or so) at a time, sticking on the elder flowers as you go. Arrange the flowers as evenly as possible and take care to avoid straight lines (*below*).

3 Arrange the flowers within each compartment. Any small flowers will do, but if you have fewer kinds than the number of ogee compartments, be sure to place them symmetrically.

4 The stems of each flower cluster are made from thin pieces of moss. (Note that the annual phlox flowers do not have stems.)

5 Place pieces of moss in the four corners of the picture.

QUEEN ANNE'S LACE FAN

Even Queen Anne would surely have approved of this exquisite floral fan based on Queen Anne's lace flowers. The delicate blues of speedwell and cornflowers are set off by subtle beiges and browns radiating out from a bright yellow leopard's-bane flower.

Picture size
250 x 330mm (10 x 14in)

You will need
White cardboard
Ruler
Pencil
Pair of compasses
Protractor (optional)
PVA (white) glue
Small paintbrush
Tweezers
Pencil eraser

Plant material
1 Leopard's-bane (pressed in profile)
2 Perennial cornflower
3 Sorrel
4 Elder
5 Gorse
6 Queen Anne's lace or cow parsley
7 Speedwell
8 Sycamore

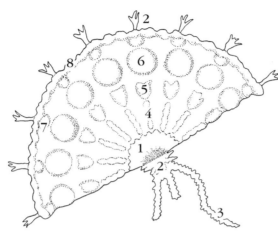

The fully semi-circular fan first appeared at the beginning of the eighteenth century, during the reign of Queen Anne. Before then the usual shape for a fan was a quarter-circle. The best fans were very often made of delicately carved ivory, with lace or silk, and were sometimes encrusted with jewels set in gold or silver.

A single leopard's-bane flower in profile makes an eminently suitable central cardinal point and handle of this fan design. The fan sticks are represented by lines of single elder flowers. Then on each segment comes a gorse blossom, followed by a single spray of Queen Anne's lace or cow-parsley umbellifer. This in turn is surmounted by a solitary speedwell flower.

The outer edge is composed of greenish-yellow sycamore flowers, so abundant in their season and so often despised by over-fussy pressed-flower artists. The outermost fringe features perennial cornflower petals, echoed by the cornflower bow at the handle, which has a ribbon of sorrel flower spikes. The whole picture, with its subtle combination of pastel shades, has a cool, lacy look.

1 Sort through your flower selection and divide them into groups of each type of flower, discarding any that are damaged.

2 Lightly pencil in the fan shape on the cardboard, using a ruler and compasses, and a protractor if desired. Mark a point halfway along the curve, and mark two points equally spaced between them, so that the semi-circle is divided into quarters. (If you are using a protractor, the points will be at 45°, 90° and 135° on the protractor.)

3 Brush the curving line with PVA (white) glue. Using tweezers, position the sycamore flowers (*below*). It is easiest to paste and stick only a few centimetres (an inch or so) at a time, so that the glue will not dry before you have finished sticking on the flowers.

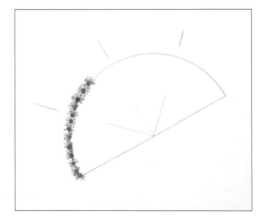

4 Once you have positioned all the sycamore flowers, fix three Queen Anne's lace (or cow parsley) umbels evenly beneath your three marked points on the curve.

5 Fix the leopard's-bane flower in place at the centre of the semi-circle (*below*).

6 Take four more Queen Anne's lace umbels and glue them on either side of the first three, forming an arc inside the sycamore flower curve. Erase the base line and then glue the two remaining Queen Anne's lace umbels in place.

7 Erase the remaining pencil marks, and position the gorse blossoms, placing one flower under each of the Queen Anne's lace umbels and once again forming an arc.

8 Arrange the elder flowers in straight lines, radiating out from the centre, like the sticks of the fan, with one line leading to each gorse flower.

9 Glue speedwell flowers just inside the sycamore flowers, with one speedwell flower centred over each Queen Anne's lace umbel.

10 Beyond each speedwell flower, on the outer edge, add a cornflower petal to look like fringe.

11 Finally, glue some sorrel at the base to make "ribbons" and some more cornflower petals to form a "bow".

GOLDEN PHEASANT

Not only does this spectacular picture of a pheasant really look like a pheasant, but it also shows off to best advantage every one of the beautiful pressed flowers and leaves of which it is comprised, particularly the sweet william petals that make up the breast plumage.

Picture size
220 x 330mm (8⅝ x 13in)

You will need
Black cardboard
Thin white paper
Pencil
Scissors
PVA (white) glue
Small paintbrush
Tweezers

Plant material
1 Sweet william petals
2 Foxglove leaf
3 Alstroemeria petals
4 Hypericum petal
5 Hypericum stamens
6 Dianthus petals
7 Ox-eye daisy petals
8 Buttercups
9 Yorkshire fog grass heads
10 Mugwort young leaves
11 Perennial cornflower petals
12 Elder flower and part of foxglove petal

Sweet williams often have dark crimson, white-edged petals, but they are chunky flowers, too awkward to be pressed in their entirety. Pressed separately, however, these petals make perfect fluffy feathers. Here they look convincing as the breast plumage of this ornamental bird.

Part of a foxglove leaf, showing the intricate vein system of its underside, forms the wing. The rump and tail feathers are alstroemeria petals. The undertail feathers are white dianthus and ox-eye daisy.

The head is a hypericum petal, and the crest a cluster of hypericum stamens. The gold mantle is buttercup, pressed with heat to produce this dark amber shade.

The sweeping tail is Yorkshire fog grass. Other grasses may do equally well, but because dried grass tends to fall to bits eventually, the completed picture will really need lamination or an adhesive cover. This means that the bulkier grasses should be avoided. Yorkshire fog is the right colour, and has just the right feathery appearance without the bulk.

Touches of blue here and there are provided by the feathery petals of perennial

garden cornflower. The feet are the naturally formed leaf-claws of mugwort – the youngest leaves that cling tightly to the upper part of the stem.

Finally, a touch of foxglove petal forms the facial mask, while the eye consists of a solitary elder flower.

Buttercups intended to represent feathers are best pressed in profile – that is, with the flowers "closed". When ready to be used, the petals, complete with stamens, are separated in one piece from the calyx and stem by holding them between thumb and forefinger, and giving a sharp tug.

1 Draw or trace the pheasant on a separate piece of paper and use it as a guide to try out petals for size and fit.

2 Black cardboard gives dramatic contrast, but you may find that the buttercups in particular have become translucent enough for them to lose colour against the black backing. If this happens, cut the shape of the bird's mantle out of thin white paper and stick it in place first, as a base for the flowers. You *could* cut out and glue on the entire body shape in this way, if you find it easier. But you will then need to align the petal edges very carefully with the edge of the paper, or the feathery effect will be lost.

3 Position the sweet william breast feathers next, commencing at the tail end so that they overlap naturally. Above them, also beneath the tail, place the ox-eye daisy petals (*below*).

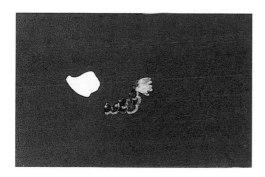

4 The ox-eye daisy petals are over-lapped by the white dianthus petals, which are overlapped in their turn by the alstroemeria over-tail coverts. Now position the foxglove leaf wing.

5 Select a hypericum petal with an appropriately "beaky" base, if necessary bending it to shape. Insert the bunch of hypericum stamens to form the crest.

6 Position the grass tail, making sure that it appears to grow from beneath the tail covert feathers, without actually making an unsightly bulge (*below*).

7 Select suitable unfolded young mug-wort leaves to form the legs and feet. Trim them with scissors if necessary.

8 Arrange the cornflower petals in twos and threes to add the finishing touches.

SPIT, BANE AND WORT

This cheerful picture has the same fresh, unsophisticated charm as a posy of wild flowers. More than a dozen wild flowers are incorporated into the design, most of them with names that conjure up the herbal lore of country folk from centuries gone by.

Picture size
310 x 420mm (12 x 16½in)

You will need
Heavy paper in medium green
PVA (white) glue
Small paintbrush
Tweezers

Plant material
1 Yellow spit (greater celandine)
2 Fleabane
3 Mugwort
4 Devil's milk (wood spurge)
5 Stinging nettle
6 Woundwort
7 Dog's mercury
8 Figwort
9 Nipplewort
10 Hemlock
11 Spearmint
12 Water mint
13 Pilewort (lesser celandine)

The names of some of our wild plants recall the herb culture of long ago. Some of these old names are fairly general – woundwort, for instance, was used for healing wounds – but some are more specific.

Figwort was so-named after the shape of the tiny seed-cases, but it was used medicinally as a cure for "king's evil", or scrofula. The best-known "cure" for this ailment was the personal touch of a king or queen – Queen Anne was the last British monarch to practise it – but the herbal remedy was probably more efficacious, and certainly much more readily accessible.

Stinging nettles were also used medicinally: as a counter-irritant, to take the patient's mind off more serious problems; as a counteractive agent for wasp (but not for bee) stings; and in "urtication" – flogging with a bunch of nettles – which was

recommended as providing relief for rheumatic stiffness.

Then there is pilewort, the old name for lesser celandine. "Celandine" is a far more romantic name (it comes from the Norman French *celidoine*, meaning a swallow) which really ought to belong only to greater celandine, as it blooms nearer the time of the swallows' visit. Greater celandine, which is not so valuable for pressing as lesser celandine, was called "yellow spit" – its yellow sap was used to treat warts.

Fleabane was formerly used as an insect repellent, and the smell of the crushed leaves is said to keep fleas away. But original meanings sometimes become lost. Mugwort ought more correctly to be "midge-wort" (Anglo-Saxon *mucgwyrt*), as this or some related plant of the wormwood family was used as a remedy against midge bites.

Hint

• *Trying to make a coherent design out of an assortment of oddly shaped pieces of vegetation that lack showy flowers can stretch one's ingenuity to new lengths. The first decision to make is a basic one: whether to aim for a believable piece of scenery – a landscape – or to settle for a centrally pivoted design and work towards making a pleasing pattern.*

Another wild plant in this picture is the wood spurge. The name "spurge" comes from a Norman French word meaning "to purge". In the sixteenth century it was known as "devil's milk". Most plants of the spurge family have medicinal uses for their thick, milky, poisonous sap. Other deadly poisonous herbs are the dog's mercury and hemlock. In contrast to these, the two wild mints are greatly valued for their flavour.

If the picture is to be a landscape, then there is the problem of how to dispose of all those loose ends. Do you leave them floating unanchored in space, or do you conceal each one behind another sprig?

This picture represents just one possible solution, using the separated flowers of pilewort (lesser celandine) and fleabane to form a "woodland carpet". These flowers relate reasonably well to the make-believe horizon, which crosses the picture about two-thirds of the way up from the base. The long sprays of tiny flowers spear quite happily into the sky space, bolstered up both by their own foliage and by that of the other plants.

1 With such a varied assortment of wild plants, there is no way you can copy a design exactly. All you can do is follow

the general rules of composition. Start with the tallest and slenderest plants at each side, rearranging them without sticking them down, and trying various bulkier plants at their base until you feel you have found an agreeable balance (*below left*).

2 Infill with your remaining plants, starting always at the top and working downwards, planning to conceal any loose ends. Mugwort leaves and fleabane flowers are ideal for this purpose. Do not glue anything down until you are certain that the composition is the way you want it (*below*).

3 Think of the picture as a landscape with a horizon (your eye-level), foreground and background, with the tallest plants representing trees. Now place the smaller flowers at ground level. Never use small infill plants above your imaginary horizon, or the result will be clutter.

CHINESE LILY VASE

*Dramatic Peruvian lilies and modest sprigs of stitchwort complement
each other perfectly on this splendid vase. Based on antique Chinese
porcelain from around a thousand years ago, the vase is first given
highlights and shadows using pastel crayon.*

This design was inspired by antique porcelain from the Sung Dynasty (960–1279), the golden age of Chinese flower painting. The original vase would probably have featured native Chinese tiger lilies, but as these are rather too large for this, small hybrid Peruvian lilies have been used. Because the lily foliage is too shrubby, daffodil leaves are used instead.

An unobtrusive "filler" is needed to complement the theme, and sprigs of stitchwort are ideal. The tiny white flowers become somewhat transparent after pressing, while the leaves and stems form a faint tracery which fills the vacant ground without detracting from the main subject.

The picture only really works if careful attention is paid to highlight and shadow, otherwise the vase will look flat.

1 Enlarge the template on page 72 by 133 per cent on a photocopier. Transfer it to cardboard or thin plastic sheet. Cut out and use as a stencil for each half of the vase. This will prevent you from going over the edge with the soft pastel, which is difficult to remove cleanly.

2 Position the stencil on the cardboard and hold it in place while you apply the colour, using the side of the crayon. Colour in the vase only lightly so that the background colour shows through. In this way the final colour of the vase will be a paler version of the background, and will not clash with it. For the shadow at the edges, use pale umber (*below*), darkening to black at the base and beneath the lip of the vase.

(steps continued overleaf)

Picture size
*390 x 260mm (15¼ x
10¼in)*

You will need
Dark-coloured cardboard
*Cardboard or thin plastic
sheet for stencil*
Pencil
Scissors
*Pastel crayon in white,
pale umber and black*
PVA (white) glue
Small paintbrush
Tweezers

Plant material
1 Peruvian lily flowers
2 Daffodil leaves
3 Stitchwort sprigs

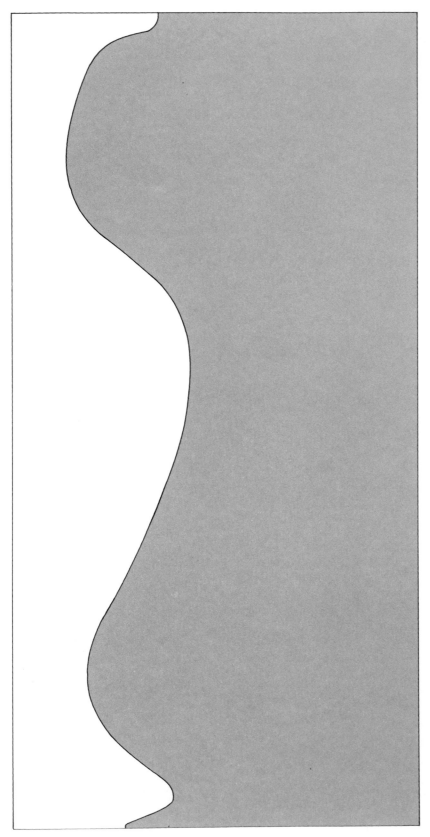

3 Position the Peruvian lilies and the foliage. In this case, leaves are playing the role of stems, and the base of each flower should seem to rise from the leaf nodes. Make the curves appear natural, more or less in harmony with the curve of the vase (*below*).

4 Add the sprigs of stitchwort wherever they seem to be needed. Trim odd pieces and tips of petal and leaf so that they fit neatly at the edges and seem to emerge from around the side of the vase. Conceal the base of the lily "stems" beneath a broader leaf tip encircling the base of the vase.

SUNLIT VASE OF FLOWERS

Sunlight floods this picture of a glass vase filled with delicate flowers, inspired by seventeenth-century Spanish flower paintings. The predominant yellow and orange tones create the perfect background for the vivid blues and mauves of cornflower and mallow.

Picture size
460 x 350mm (18 x 13¾in)

You will need
Yellow cardboard
Pastel crayons in white, green, burnt umber, orange and burnt sienna
PVA (white) glue
Small paintbrush
Tweezers

Plant material
1 Musk mallow
2 Common mallow
3 Cornflower (pressed without their hard centres, then reassembled)
4 Bird's-foot trefoil
5 Alstroemeria
6 Yellow iris
7 Old-man's-beard
8 Cut-leaved geranium

lines of the stiffly upright stems and leaves softened by the trailing pendulous material overlying the curve of the vase.

1 On the yellow cardboard, draw the vase and colour it in using white pastel highlighted with dabs of colour. Draw in the table top, and the reflection of the vase on the polished surface, using burnt umber and white. As always, care is needed to place the base of the vase firmly on the table, particularly as the downward reflection of the glass precludes the use of heavy shadow at the base. If desired, shade in the yellow background using orange darkening to burnt sienna (*below*).

Here, the aim is to give the impression of strong light shining on and through the glass vase and flowers. The flowers are all light and not too solidly petalled, and the backing is pale yellow so the light appears to shine through the petals. The small yellow irises at the top, which are slightly darker than the backing, may fade until they are paler than it, but no matter. A ghostlike translucency adds to the effect of intense light.

The picture was inspired by the paintings of the seventeenth century Spanish painter Juan de Arellano (1614–1672) who produced many masterpieces of flower-painting technique. His containers tended to be arranged with long stems and overhanging trails, stressing the free and easy growth of the flowers. Most of Arellano's flower arrangements are tall and thin, with the outlines

2 Arrange the reassembled cornflowers (pressed without their hard centres) to their best advantage. After all the

trouble of making them up, it would
be a shame to lose sight of them in a
jumble of vegetation.

3 Now position the long spearing
leaves, making sure that they seem to
rise naturally from inside the vase (*left*).

4 Position the pendulous bird's-foot
trefoil flowers, and finally fill in with the
remaining plant material.

5 When the design is complete, you can
add a few finishing touches of pastel to
represent reflections.

6 Take care that the fallen petals seem
to lie firmly on the table top. A touch of
pastel shadow beneath them can add to
the illusion of solidity.

MOUNT LU IN MISTY RAIN

*Inspired by an ancient Chinese poem, this picture is a good example of
how one plant – in this case, rosebay willowherb, which provided flowers,
foliage and seed-down – can sometimes provide enough interest and
variety to form the basis of an entire scene.*

Picture size
*350 x 260mm (13¾ x
10¼in)*

You will need
*Yellow cardboard
Laminating film or self-
adhesive plastic film
Tweezers
Glass paint in green
(optional)*

Plant material
*1 Rosebay willowherb
flowers
2 Rosebay willowherb
and old-man's-beard
seed-down
3 Rosebay willowherb
leaf
4 Azalea petals
5 Moss*

The starting point for this picture was an
ancient Chinese poem:

*Mount Lu in misty rain, the river Che in
spate.
While I was away, I knew no rest from
longing...*

Whether it succeeds or not as a Chinese-
style picture, it certainly demonstrates the
versatility of the ubiquitous rosebay willowherb. This plant, which is common in
Asia as well as Europe and North America,
supplied the flowers, the leafy boat, the
clouds of seed-down surrounding the
mountain, and the foaming waves of the
flooded river.

The higher splashing waves are old-
man's-beard (wild clematis), which also helps
to delineate the clouds. The boatman is part
of an azalea flower, but almost any oddly
shaped fragment might have done the job.
The rest of the picture is made with moss

of various kinds, and finished with a smear
of colour here and there.

Seed-down is not easy to handle, and if
you are laminating a picture such as this,
or providing it with a self-adhesive plastic
film, you will find the job almost impossible if you follow the conventional method.
Sticky film is difficult to apply to pressed
flowers at the best of times – it sticks
where it touches, and unless you are lucky
enough to get it right first time, the picture
will be ruined. Static electricity makes mat-
ters worse, causing petals to curl and fluffy
material to fly upwards. The more you try
to retrieve and adjust it, the worse the
problem becomes.

To prevent loose material flying around,
or adhesive film sticking in the wrong
places, the solution is to assemble the picture in reverse – face down on a sheet of
film, with the backing applied last. After
smoothing down or heat-pressing, the job
is done, apart from trimming or folding over
the margins. This method is also suitable
for small, simple designs – cards, bookmarks
and the like.

1 Plan your design and arrange it
directly on the backing cardboard, without sticking anything down at this stage.
Cut the protective film to size and place
it, contact side up, next to your design.

2 Only when you are completely satisfied start carefully transferring the items,
one at a time and face downwards, onto
the upturned film, using tweezers and
your fingertips. Glue is obviously not
necessary, but a sudden draught at this
stage could prove disastrous. First position the seed-down for the foam and
clouds, then add the moss.

3 Now put on the rosebay willowherb leaf for the boat, and the rosebay willowherb flowers for the tree (*right*).

4 Add the azalea petal for the boatman's hat, a piece of stem for the oar, and then the azalea petal for the boatman.

5 Finally, position a piece of ivy-leaved toadflax or other trailing material for the trunk of the flowering tree.

6 Place the backing cardboard over all, and smooth down firmly before inverting. The result is a mirror image of your original design. As the picture is now safely covered, you can if desired add a smear of green glass paint here and there to make the mountain and the river banks look more solid.

LIGHT AND SHADE

Surrounded by atmospheric shadows, the brilliantly coloured flowers of this dramatic still-life seem to radiate light. The picture, which was inspired by the flower paintings of the Flemish artist Jan Breughel, fully exploits the possibilities of light and shade.

Picture size

350 x 460mm (13¾ x 18in)

You will need

Black mountboard
Pastel crayons in white, grey, sap green and Hooker's green
PVA (white) glue
Small paintbrush
Tweezers
Glass paint in dark blue or brown (optional)

Plant material

1 Pelargonium centred with meadowsweet
2 Larkspur
3 Hydrangea centred with sycamore
4 Annual phlox
5 Potentilla fruticosa
6 Meadowsweet
7 Ramsons
8 Montbretia
9 Honeysuckle
10 Snapdragon

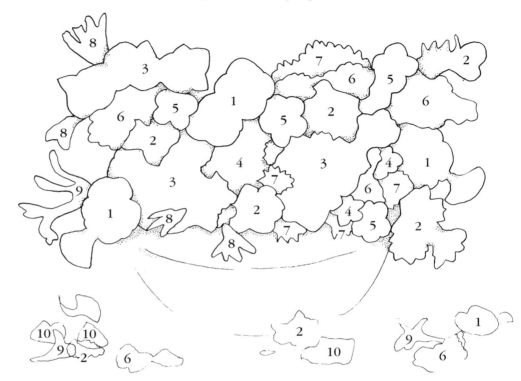

Jan Breughel (1569–1625) pioneered the painting of flowers in their own right, rather than as mere decorations for religious subjects. In his beautiful, velvety pictures (he is sometimes called "Breughel de velours") he loved to explore the chiaroscuro effect, using a simple dark background against which his flowers seemed to glow with light. The darker outer edges of his arrangements would merge with the heavy shadows beyond, making the centre of the group seem to stand out in high relief.

Breughel's pupil Daniel Seghers (1590–1661) produced marvellous work in a similar vein. For mastery of composition and colour, and sensitive treatment of light and shade, the quality of Breughel's and Seghers's work has seldom been surpassed to this day.

Much the same approach to handling light and shade is used in this pressed-flower picture. The bowl itself is barely seen in the shadows. One has to imagine that the flowers are illuminated not by electric light or gas, but rather by a bank of candles or, at best, a flickering seventeenth-century oil lamp. To obtain this effect, black mountboard has been used.

The darkest flowers have been used at the edges of the arrangement, apart from the dark interval to divide the centre. Where the flowers did not seem dark enough to give the desired effect, shadow was added with dark glass paint after the work was laminated.

Full use is made of the slightly rough-grained surface of the black mountboard to catch flecks of pastel, suggesting antique glazed pottery where light strikes the sides of the bowl.

1 Draw the bowl, using the side of a soft pastel crayon, pressing gently so as to emphasize the grain of the mount-board. The bowl is suggested by white and grey pastel with indentations in sap-green pastel around the rim, and a few dabs of Hooker's green pastel to create highlights.

2 Decide the upward and outward limits of your arrangement, positioning the cornermost flowers first.

3 Now map out the darker shadowy areas at the sides and the centre of the arrangement. Don't forget that the light-est, brightest flowers will need to overlap the darker ones in order to give the picture depth.

4 Position the main highlighted groups (*above right*). Add any finishing touches such as fallen petals.

5 Tuck the smaller edging flowers, montbretia, honeysuckle, and ramsons, slightly beneath neighbouring petals. Use sprigs of meadowsweet and any odd small flowers to fill gaps.

6 If, after laminating, the flowers at the edge do not seem dark enough, add a few shadows with smears of bluish or brownish glass paint.

GARDEN WICKET

This fresh and spontaneous flower "doodle" provides good practice not only in achieving a balanced design but in exploring combinations of flowers and finding out what goes with what. It is also a good way to use up any odd flowers and trailing tips.

Picture size
390 x 260mm (15¼ x 10¼in)

You will need
Yellow cardboard
Silvery-grained Japanese wood veneer-faced paper
Scissors
PVA (white) glue
Small paintbrush
Pastel crayons in sap green and white
Tweezers

Plant material
1 Cottongrass (centred with hawkbit)
2 Larkspur
3 Pelargonium (one centred with yellow alyssum)
4 Musk mallow (centred with yellow alyssum)
5 Common mallow
6 Bird's-foot trefoil
7 Buttercup
8 Heuchera
9 Fuchsia
10 Crocosmia
11 Bluebell
12 Field bindweed

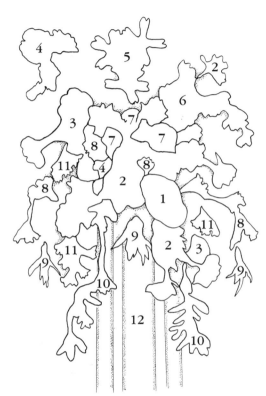

Trails of the small field bindweed grow up the wicket, some of these blossoming unexpectedly into a riot of colour. Many of the flowers are eccentric composites: for example, musk mallow and pelargonium centred with yellow alyssum; and cotton-grass centred with hawkbit. But this is not intended as a botanist's plant portrait, merely an excuse for a tangle of trailing growth and pendulous flowers.

1 Using scissors, cut the veneer-faced paper into three 190mm (7⅜in) long strips, with two of them 15mm (⅝in) wide and one 30mm (1¼in) wide.

2 Glue the veneer-paper strips on the yellow cardboard, with the wider one in the centre. Give them the appearance of solidity by adding green pastel crayon along the long edges and a highlight of white pastel crayon down the centre of each. Smear with your fingertip.

3 Position the twisting trails of bind-weed on the strips and stick them in place. Arrange the outermost flowers and foliage as a guide *(below)*. Do not glue them permanently until you are quite satisfied that the picture will hang together coherently.

4 Position the largest central flowers, and work outwards from these, fitting in the intermediaries to link the design together. Add the pendulous flowers and any trailing tips for balance.

A THOUSAND BLOSSOMS

*Its title notwithstanding, this early-spring scene is simplicity itself to make.
Just three types of flower, some Japanese wood veneer-faced paper,
a few strips of moss and a little pastel are all that's needed to create a
believable landscape.*

Picture size
355 x 456mm (14 x 18in)

You will need
*Black mountboard
Japanese wood veneer-
    faced paper
Pencil
Scissors
PVA (white) glue
Small paintbrush
Pastel crayons in moss
    green and white*

Plant material
*1 Hawkbit
2 Annual phlox
3 Flowering currant
    (Ribes sanguineum)
4 Moss (and fallen
    blossom)*

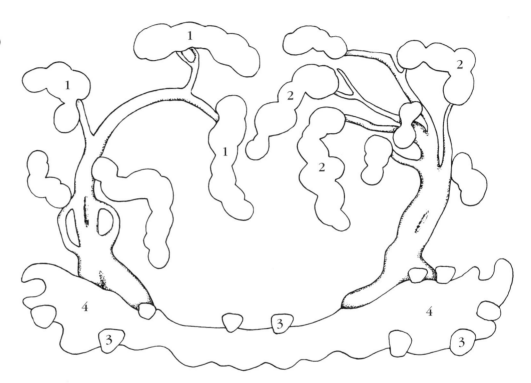

The inspiration for this picture was a verse from Omar Khayyam:

*And look – a thousand blossoms with the
    day
Woke – and a thousand scatter'd into clay.*

The two gnarled trees have been cut out of thin wood veneer-faced paper. The veneer has been given solidity with an outline of moss-green pastel, and also provided with extended root buttresses to suggest a flowing contour.

The poet's thousand blossoms are, on the left-hand tree, hawkbit and, on the right-hand one, annual phlox, falling together among the tiny trumpets of flowering currant which is growing through the moss. Leaves on the trees would have been superfluous.

1 Draw the shape of the trees lightly on the reverse side of the Japanese wood veneer, taking care not to damage the paper-thin veneer. Remember that the two trees should curve in opposite directions. Extra branches and root buttresses can be cut out of the pieces of veneer, which would otherwise be wasted.

2 Glue the trees to the mountboard, inserting the ends of the extra pieces slightly underneath the main tree trunk, and trimming them as necessary, in order to give a natural appearance. Remember that flowing lines are important in this type of picture.

3 The trees can be given a realistically solid appearance by edging them with

moss-green pastel crayon, and adding a touch of white highlight down the centre of each tree. Smear this pastel slightly with your fingertip – always in the direction of tree growth, and never across the grain.

4 When you are satisfied with the trees and their roots, add the strands of moss to represent the ground – a broad, sweeping vista seen between the trees.

5 Position the ground vegetation (the flowering currant) in the moss (*above right*). Place the blossoms loosely at first before you start gumming them in place. You may want to conceal the branch ends, but at the same time it is important to avoid overcrowding. Try

not to space them too regularly – imagine they are being tossed by a spring breeze. As they fall from the trees they will be caught by this gentle breeze and wafted in a slight curve before settling on the mossy ground.

BLUE LOTUS

This picture is a good example of the value of not trying to cram too much into one picture. A delphinium and a larkspur flower depict a single water lily, and watery reflections are added by hand. It is intended to make a pair with "Tree on a Hillside" (see pages 86 – 7).

Picture size
200 x 160mm (8 x 6¼in)

You will need
*Light blue mottled board
    or wallpaper mounted
    on cardboard
Crayons, coloured
    pencils, or paintbrush
    and watercolour paints,
    in turquoise, purple-
    blue, green and brown
PVA (white) glue
Small paintbrush
Tweezers*

Plant material
*1 Delphinium
2 Larkspur
3 Jack-by-the-hedge
    (common garlic
    mustard) leaves
4 Spider plant leaves*

Several different flowers could be used to portray the water lily, and various "lotus flowers" feature in the religious mythology of the East. The true blue lotus was known to the ancient Egyptians. Revered as the sacred flower of the Nile, it was a traditional motif of their art and architecture.

Our own version of this exotic water lily is an amalgam of a delphinium and a larkspur flower, with leaves of Jack-by-the-hedge, the common garlic mustard. The pointed leaves representing reeds – papyrus, perhaps – are spider plant, but any similar-shaped leaves would do as well.

It is an easy picture to make, but would not really work without the water and the reflections being added by hand.

1 First draw a purple-blue waterline almost halfway up the picture – this will leave enough room both for the leaves and for their reflections. Hold a ruler firmly in place along the waterline, and paint or crayon a narrow turquoise line along the bottom side of the purple-blue line. With the ruler still in place, wash or smear the turquoise line a little to give a watery effect, taking care not to smear it above the waterline.

2 Construct your lotus flower on a separate piece of paper if you find it easier. It consists of a single delphinium, centred by a smaller larkspur. A touch of glue at this stage will hold the larkspur flower in place. Fold the lowest delphinium petal up so it partially hides the larkspur, and fix in place with another dab of glue. Now transfer the completed lotus to the board or paper so that it sits on the waterline (*below*).

3 Fold the garlic mustard leaves so that they too seem to sit on the water, tucking them slightly beneath the outer delphinium petals (*left*).

4 Trim the bases of the spider plant leaves to fit, and glue them in place at the waterline.

5 Add reflections, again using paint or crayon. Make sure that the reflections are more or less equal and opposite to their leaves and petals.

TREE ON A HILLSIDE

There is more than a hint of bonsai in this gnarled little tree depicted in the Oriental style. Simple and charming, the picture is made from forget-me-nots and moss, combined with veneer-faced paper. It is intended to be paired with "Blue Lotus" (see pages 84–5).

Picture size
200 x 160mm (8 x 6¼in)

You will need
Orangey-beige mottled cardboard or wallpaper mounted on cardboard
Japanese wood veneer-faced paper (or coloured paper) in deep brown
Scissors
PVA (white) glue
Small paintbrush
Tweezers
Pastel crayons in moss green and light brown (optional)

Plant material
1 Forget-me-nots
2 Fine, ferny moss
3 Coarse, trailing moss

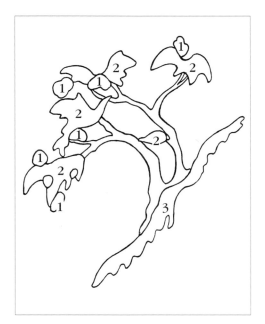

The twin tree "trunks" can be made of almost anything you have to hand – in this case, scrap offcuts of thin veneer-faced paper cut into suitably wavy, tapering shapes. A fine ferny moss provides foliage, with two or three clusters of forget-me-not to accentuate the curving outline, and add a subdued touch of colour complementary to the mottled orangey-beige of the backing board.

The hillside on which the tree is growing is simply a strand or two of a different sort of moss. This should be sufficient to create the illusion, but if what it is meant to be is not apparent, the solid hillside can always be coloured in later.

1 Using scissors, make the twin tree stems, cutting them out from a piece of veneer-faced paper or any suitably coloured piece of paper. If you are using veneer, try to cut the stems so that the direction of the wood grain more or less follows the direction of stem growth. Arrange the tree on the backing first before sticking it down, bearing in mind the slope of the hill and the spread of the foliage, to obtain a well-balanced picture. Now glue it in place.

2 Select and position the long strips of moss, facing downwards, to represent the hillside (*below*).

3 Add the tufts of ferny moss to represent storm-tossed foliage. Now glue on small clumps of forget-me-nots. Take care not to overdo the flowers, or the tree may look top-heavy.

4 If desired, use the moss-green and light brown pastel crayons to add a little colour to the hillside.

DESIGN FOR A CEILING

The floral motifs often found on enriched plaster ceilings in stately homes of bygone years were the starting point for this design, consisting of wild yarrow heads and three kinds of leaves. The picture demonstrates that bright colours are not essential to make an interesting study.

Picture size
300 x 320mm (11¾ x 12½in)

You will need
Cream-coloured paper or board
Pencil
Pair of compasses, or two round objects approximately 120mm (4¾in) and 105mm (4in) in diameter
PVA (white) glue
Small paintbrush
Tweezers

Plant material
1 Yarrow heads
2 Silverweed leaves
3 Mugwort leaves
4 Cerastium leaves

Small flowers and leaves in white, cream and grey sometimes have a texture reminiscent of antique plaster, and this design was inspired by one of the plaster ceiling panels in the Great Hall of Syon House in West London.

Wild yarrow heads are seldom of very much use to the pressed-flower artist, except perhaps for the pink variety, and this pale garlanded motif provides an excellent chance to use some of the white ones to good effect; their curving outline suits the smoothly curving design.

The motif in the centre circle is a cluster of mugwort, topped with a yarrow head. The leaves within the quatrefoils are silverweed, and those beyond the four corners of the design are cerastium.

1 Lightly pencil in the circles on the paper or board, using compasses or any suitably sized round objects as a guide. The central circle and two side circles are each 120mm (4¾in) in diameter, and the other two are 105mm (4in) in diameter. They overlap so that the

actual motif is about 270mm (10½in) from side to side, and the same from top to bottom.

2 It is now a simple matter to glue the yarrow heads in position symmetrically, using their natural shape to accentuate the curves.

3 Glue on the silverweed next, tucking each stem slightly beneath the yarrow to conceal loose ends.

4 Position the mugwort leaves in the middle of the design, with all their stems approximately at the centre of the circle (*below*). You will probably need five or six leaves.

5 Use the roundest yarrow head you can find to centre the mugwort leaves and conceal their loose ends, providing the central boss.

6 Select narrow sprigs of cerastium or other grey or silver leaves to fit in the four corners. Glue in place.

PATTERN SAMPLE BOOKMARKS

The inconsequential gift of a simple bookmark is a good excuse to demonstrate your skill at pattern making. Art Nouveau, Art Deco, and even Art Trouvé (see page 21) can all feature strongly in your original designs, which can be either symmetrical or asymmetrical.

Picture size (each)
220 x 60mm (8⅝ x 2¼in)

You will need
*Black or white thin
  cardboard
Craft knife, to cut
  cardboard
PVA (white) glue
Small paintbrush
Tweezers*

Plant material
*1 Woodruff leaves
2 Lawn daisy
3 Buttercup
4 Aubrieta flowers
5 Moss
6 Montbretia
7 Birch leaves
8 Fern frond
9 Fuchsia flower
10 Small leaves or sprigs*

Repetitive designs, though simple, need careful planning if they are to look really effective. They may feature the familiar – rearranged – or the strikingly unusual. Regular symmetry in the plant world is unusual, and when it occurs it lends itself very readily to this style of picture.

A few sprigs of woodruff will give you a collection of interesting shapes. Each nine-petalled green "flower" may be clipped clean of the stem and, as in this case, centred with a solitary lawn daisy, like some exotic green-sepalled bloom – an ideal starting-shape for a semi-formal design. A brightly contrasting touch of orangey-yellow is provided by the bordering buttercups. Their profile setting, by doubling the petal thickness, intensifies their colour against the white ground.

Another symmetrically repetitive design is provided by four little clusters of aubrieta, with the addition of a few twists of moss to give a delightfully ferny effect. The true leaves of the main subject would have been too heavy for the design.

A non-symmetrical design is provided by the largely reconstructed spike of montbretia, again demonstrating the happy blend of orange and light green against a white backing. Two sprigs of silver birch leaves plus a fern frond complete a well-balanced design which could, if desired, repeat itself endlessly in a larger and more complicated format.

Fuchsias against a black background can look quite striking as a repetitive pattern. The leaves again are not their own, as they would have been too large.

1 Make sprigs of two, three or four separate aubrieta flowers and apply glue to the cardboard rather than the petals, which are notorious for rolling themselves up into a messy ball. Press them firmly in place. Moss can be added as you proceed or after the design is complete.

2 You will probably need to try several different montbretia tips and individual flowers before you find ones which arc of the right size and spread to fit your card, as montbretia does vary greatly. The same applies to the birch leaves and the fern frond used in this bookmark. Use the birch leaf sprigs alternately front and rear side uppermost for a subtle contrast.

3 Select the most symmetrical woodruff leaves. The less evenly shaped ones can be used in informal designs. It is better to apply glue to an area of cardboard and lay your material on this, rather than gluing the leaves or petals individually, as they can break. Complete gluing down is essential if the bookmark is not to be protected with transparent film.

4 Try out fuchsia flowers for uniform size and plumpness before sticking them in place. Decide whether to make use of this difference in your design, or to choose a uniform size. Any small lcaves or sprigs will do as stem-concealing supporters, and again you need to look for uniformity.

APOTHECARY'S ROSE

A radiating pattern of stems and leaves, centred by an anchoring group of crimson apothecary's roses and coupled with the use of backing shadows, gives a lively but wholly solid feel to this design, which was inspired by eighteenth-century Dutch flower paintings.

Picture size
460 x 350mm (18 x 13¾in)

You will need
Dark green textured cardboard
Cardboard or thin plastic sheet, for stencil
Scissors
Pastel crayons in muted tones to blend with flowers, such as Naples yellow, burnt sienna, and yellow ochre with titanium white (for vase), plus brown (for table) and black (for shadows)
Ruler
PVA (white) glue
Small paintbrush
Tweezers

Plant material
1 Apothecary's rose (Rosa gallica officinalis)
2 Dog rose
3 Larkspur
4 Rhododendron
5 Fuchsia
6 Goldenrod
7 Purple iris
8 Daffodil
9 Lavender

Foliage includes ivy, forsythia, bridewort, guelder rose, rose, iris, hypericum, cherry, beech, yarrow, larkspur and daffodil

One of the greatest European flower painters was the Dutchman, Jan Van Huysum (1682–1749). His flowers were unsurpassed for their three-dimensional quality, their delicate contours and combinations of colour, with contrasting light and dark flowers. His paintings were perfectly balanced, but each flower followed its own inclination, with long arching stems and trails as well as compact clusters – a scattering perhaps of loose sprays of larkspur and campanula, and stiffly erect tulips, set among clustered roses and carnations. Van Huysum's compositions were often very similar to the work of modern flower arrangers. One of his favourite devices was to place an arrangement close to a wall, where the complex shadows of the flowers could enhance the effect of depth.

This is the inspiration for this picture. It uses dark green cardboard to give the picture an antique appearance, and the effect is strengthened by the shadows of the flowers against the wall. Van Huysum was probably familiar with the old-fashioned "apothecary's rose", *Rosa gallica officinalis*, which is used here.

The vase is pastelled in first, using discreet colours that will blend rather than contrast strongly with the background. If you use textured card for your backing, it is easy to obtain the mottled antique look by applying the pastels very lightly.

The shadows are best put in last, using black pastel, and this finishing touch gives the arrangement depth. Take care to get the curve at the base of the vase to look right as it rests on the table, because believable perspective will largely depend upon this.

The whole effect is deliberately low-key, and any natural fading of the flowers should not detract from it. Reassembled spikes – in this case blue and white larkspur – can be very useful where individual flowers need to be grouped without crowding rather than being scattered at random. A few leaves or flowerheads fallen onto the tabletop add solidity.

1 Using the photograph as a guide, draw a template and transfer it to a piece of cardboard or thin plastic sheet. Cut away the shape, and use the remaining piece as a stencil. This will prevent you going over the edge with the pastel, which is difficult to remove cleanly.

2 Position the stencil on the textured cardboard and hold it in place while

(steps continued overleaf)

Hints

• *If you have a few large and showy flowers which have pressed well and kept their colour, but do not seem to blend with the rest of your selection, a vase arrangement of this kind is one of the most effective ways to make good use of them and show them off to their best advantage. It is also an excellent opportunity to use assorted leaves and odd sprigs of foliage.*

• *Weedy little flowers which would look disproportionately small on their own, can often be assembled very effectively as composites, or arranged in long curving sprays, both of which fit very readily into a vase theme.*

you apply the colour. Use a short piece of pastel for preference, applied flat on its side, holding it firmly against the edge of the stencil. Apply the pastel very lightly to achieve the mottled effect. Using the darkest colour (in this case the burnt umber) towards the edge of the vase, and the lightest colour (here, the pale tint of yellow ochre) to highlight the centre will give it a more rounded, three-dimensional look. Still holding the stencil in place, smear the colour evenly with your finger.

3 Next, add the surface of the table in deep brown. Experiment with a ruler until you find the most believable level. Curve and darken the base of the vase, taking care over this so that it looks as realistic as possible (*below*). It is shading like this that creates a sense of depth.

4 Position the outermost flowers and leaves first, to help you keep a symmetrical arrangement. Assemble the spikes of larkspur at this stage, as these are the main balancing points for the design. Glue them down as soon as you are satisfied that the outline of the design is truly symmetrical (*below*).

5 Infill with the remaining plants, gluing down as you go and taking care to avoid loose ends.

6 Add the pendant fuchsias and, as a finishing touch, the fallen leaves and flowers on the table.

7 Shadows can be put in now alongside the plants and vase. Apply the black pastel very carefully to avoid damaging your plant material.

MAIL ORDER SUPPLIERS

The following suppliers offer a range of specialist materials and equipment for pressing flowers, making pictures from them and framing the pictures, as well as components for other methods of presentation such as paperweights and greetings cards. All supply by mail order.

Country Collections
Unit 9, Ditton Priors Trading Estate,
Bridgnorth, Shropshire WV16 6SS
(Pressed-flower laminating service, wooden frames, hand-engraved crystal paperweight blanks, wooden bowls with lid blanks, backing cardboard and Japanese wood-veneer paper in small sizes)

Craft Creations
*Unit 5, Harper's Yard, Ruskin Road,
London N17 8NE*
(Greetings card blanks, sealing film and boxes, bookmark blanks, full range of backing papers and cardboard)

Framecraft
*148-150 High Street, Aston,
Birmingham B6 4US*
(Wood and metal frames and holders in all shapes and sizes, dressing table sets, bowls, jars, paperweights, trays, etc, all with blank space for pressed flowers)

Impress
Slough Farm, Westhall, Halesworth,
Suffolk IP19 8RN
(Greetings card blanks, materials, pressed flowers, grasses and leaves)

Joanna Sheen Ltd
7 Lucius Street, Torquay, Devon
TQ2 5UW
(Complete range of craft components)

Paperchase
213 Tottenham Court Road, London
W1P 9AF
(An enormous range of paper, mount-board and cardboard, including Japanese wood-veneer paper)

Richard Tipper
Unit 6, Barracks Road, Sandy Lane
Trading Estate, Stourport DY13 9QB
(Complete range of frames and mounts made to order)

INDEX